Volume 11   Number 3   Spring/Summer 1994

Contents

Lincoln Review
A QUARTERLY JOURNAL

Contributing Authors to This Issue

Michael Adamson resides in San Francisco, California.

Allan C. Brownfeld is an associate editor of Lincoln Review.

Carlton L. Eugene is an architect in the greater Washington, D.C. area.

Joseph S. Fulda is with the Mount Sinai School of Medicine in New York City, New York.

Cartrell Gore lives in Brooklyn, New York.

Jason D. Hill lives in Lithonia, Georgia.

John Fulton Lewis is a contributor to Lincoln Review.

Tibor R. Machan is a professor of philosophy at Auburn University in Alabama.

Tyler Norman is a free-lance writer in Savannah, Georgia.

Gary North is president of the Institute for Christian Economics in Tyler, Texas.

J.A. Parker is editor and publisher of Lincoln Review.

W. Yvette Parker frequently contributes to Lincoln Review and lives in Alexandria, Virginia.

Edward C. Smith is an associate editor of Lincoln Review and teaches English at The American University in Washington, D.C.

Alvin Williams is an associate with the Graham Williams Group.

Editor's Comment

Self-Segregation: A Repudiation of the Vision of a Color-Blind Society

The goal of the civil rights movement in the past 70 years was to put an end to segregation and to move toward a genuinely color-blind society in which Americans would be judged as individuals and not by their race.

Now, more than forty years after school segregation was declared unconstitutional, we are confronted with a phenomenon no one expected or predicted: the growing self-segregation of minority students.

While predominantly white colleges and universities now enroll a majority of the more than 1.3 million black college students, the fact is that on many of those campuses, segregation remains alive and well. All too often, black and white students live apart, eat apart and eventually grow apart. A variety of organizations representing black, Hispanic, Asian-Americans and others seek the very kind of "separate-but-equal" privileges and facilities which the civil rights movement and men and women of goodwill of all races sought to eliminate.

"We have a campus of 25,000 students and there is no mixing across cultural and racial lines," reports Christine Romans, the editor of the student newspaper at Iowa State University. Even during a campus rally for unity after a racial incident, she reported, "all the blacks clustered together and all the whites clustered together."

A survey conducted by U.S. NEWS AND WORLD REPORT (April 19, 1993) found that 64 per cent of the editors at schools enrolling more than 10,000 students and 49 per cent of all respondents characterized the state of race relations on their campus as "fair" or "poor." Nine out

1

of 10 editors at the larger schools—75 per cent overall—reported that self-segregation among blacks was common on their campuses. The survey showed a statistically significant relationship between the degree of self-segregation by race and the number of racial incidents.

Discussing self-segregation at Duke University, Brad Rubin, editor of THE CHRONICLE, the campus daily, noted in THE LOS ANGELES TIMES (Oct. 19, 1993) that, "Duke is part of the growing trend toward, maybe even the leader of, segregated campuses . . . Whites live on the west campus, the hub of the university . . . Blacks tend to live in central-campus apartments, some distance from the . . . social scene and much less expensive. Thus, the mainstay of segregation at Duke is the same as in every big city in the nation: housing patterns . . . I live in a dorm with other white students and, like so many others, I do not make any effort to contact black students. It is the path of least resistance. I don't think they want me around, and they think I don't want them. We live with this undercurrent of tension until once in a while some event drags everyone to the racial battle lines . . . Until we have the guts and the desire to cross racial barriers and care about each other, blacks and whites on this campus will continue to develop separate cultures and live in separate worlds."

In a report on the way dormitory life reflects the trend of self-segregation on the nation's campuses, THE WASHINGTON POST (March 6, 1994) described the newest dormitory at Brown University, one set aside chiefly for black students and called Harambee House, Swahili for "the coming together of community." THE POST reported: "Several white students said they understood why there were Spanish and German Houses, because students practiced new languages there. But they said they didn't understand how there could be an 'African-American house,' because they doubted they would be allowed to have a 'White House.' Many white students were uncomfortable discussing the issue and did not want to be identified."

In February, 1994, the University of Pennsylvania's special commission studying the "key aspects of campus life" recommended that first-year students be assigned housing to avoid "self-segregation." Under the current system, students may choose where they will live. The commission found that they often "self-segregate and lose opportunities for wider interaction among diverse groups of students." Claire Fagin, Penn's interim president, said that she is considering a program for the future in which students would agree to be randomly assigned to dorms. She states: "In general, what we are seeing is a much more divided population on our college campuses. We are moving into a very, very hyphenated world: It's Asian-American, African-American . . . it's so contrary to everything I grew up with . . . when everyone fought to be just American. For many of us who stress pluralism, these are not easy times."

Discussing the racial situation at Brown, Joshua Lerner, a white sophomore, said that he had more black friends when he attended high school in Philadelphia than he does at Brown, even though he is around more black students at the present time. Lerner said that students naturally tend to eat, go to movies and parties and become friendly with the people they live with. So, he said, separate housing inhibits the mixing of different groups of people.

Columnist William Raspberry points out that, "At one school I visit every few years, I've gotten used to looking at the left side of the auditorium, a few rows from the front, to get a quick count of the black enrollment. No matter that seating is free, white students at these assemblies avoid these 'black' rows, and black students won't sit anywhere else. At other universities, the self-segregation happens in the dining hall, or at the student union. Sometimes it happens at dances, where the decision of whether to have a 'black' dance or a 'white' one is determined by choice of band or deejay. The self-segregating phenomenon goes beyond the natural desire of young people, many of them away from their hometown networks for the first time, to gravitate to those groups with whom they have most in common, or from whom they expect automatic welcome. That's part of it, of course. But much of the segregation is enforced by code expressed in some of the query: You gonna hang with us, or you gonna hang with them."

In many instances, it is colleges and universities themselves which promote the self-segregation of black students. In his book, *Inside American Education*, Thomas Sowell writes that, "Often there are social pressures, sometimes abetted by college administrators in various ways. The process begins even before the minority student sets foot on campus. Racial identity information on the admissions application form triggers racially separate listings of students, with these lists being shared with the local Black Students Union or other minority organizations on campus. Students may be invited to campus as individuals, only to discover after arrival that the gathering is all-black, all-Hispanic, etc. In short, they do not join minority organizations the way Jewish students may join Hillel or Catholics may join Newman clubs; they are *delivered* to campus minority organizations."

Mark Kathabane, a black South African author of *Kaffir Boy*, traveled to America to go to college and to escape apartheid. Instead, he discovered a voluntary kind of apartheid being practiced by black students on campus: "When I was in college, I and a few other black students were labeled Uncle Toms for sitting with whites in the cafeteria, sharing with them black culture, working with them on projects and socializing with them."

Self-segregation is not solely a black tendency but can be seen in other minorities as well. Writing in THE CARLETONIAN (Sept. 30, 1988), Keith Lee, an Asian American student at Carleton College in

3

Minnesota, reported that, "Students of color are looked down upon and sometimes openly criticized by their peers for having too many white friends, not doing enough for their respective multicultural groups, or just being too 'Americanized' or trying too hard to blend in. Using the Asian American as an example, terms like 'banana' (yellow on the outside, white on the inside) are sometimes used and questions like 'How come you don't have an Asian first name?' come up in everyday conversation."

Similarly, in an article entitled "Apartheid At Dartmouth" (THE DARTMOUTH REVIEW, Feb. 10, 1988), Harmeet Dhillon writes that the cumulative effect of self-segregation pressures eventually take their toll on minority students: "Most have a healthy attitude when they come here. They want to meet all kinds of people, and expand their intellectual and cultural horizons. Yet, if they happen to make more white friends than black ones, they quickly learn the ugly reality of Dartmouth's reverse racism. Normally-adjusted blacks are called 'in-cogs' or 'oreos,' meaning that they are 'black on the outside and white on the inside.' Most frequently, it is blacks themselves who call other blacks these hateful names. Many black freshmen can't withstand the pressure . . . They begin to eat together, live together, and join all-black fraternities and sororities . . . At first, they resisted the pressure to abandon their well-integrated circle of friends, yet were unable to keep up the resistance."

As on many campuses across the country, the Dartmouth administration encouraged and aided this process, both by arranging a special orientation weekend for blacks and by providing de facto segregated housing. Mr. Dhillon writes that, "Dartmouth participates in the segregation process by providing Cutter Hall for black housing and the Afro-American society. Although housing in Cutter is ostensibly available for anyone who wants it, the last time a white student lived there was the winter of 1986. Cutter's militant, ingrown atmosphere ensures that few whites will ever cross the threshold, let alone consider living there."

At the University of California at Berkeley, self-segregation is promoted by matching roommates by race. "I came here expecting to have friends, even room-mates of other races," a white student at Berkeley said. Of the minority students, she noted, "They go around calling everybody 'racist,' but they're the ones insisting on being separate." She added that, "If white students got together on the basis of race, they'd be considered Nazis."

Sometimes, self-segregation continues right through to the graduation ceremony itself. The Stanford CAMPUS REPORT for June 13, 1990 listed a "Black Baccalaureate," a "Native American Graduation Dinner" and an "Asian-American Graduation Reception" at separate locations.

Thomas Sowell argues that, "Because college officials respond to the organized vocal elements within each minority group, the whole racial atmosphere on campus tends to reflect the issues raised by these vocal elements and by administrators' policy responses to their charges and demands. What *most* minority students think may carry far less weight. Sad as it is to have tensions between two racial groups when they disagree, it is tragic insanity to have racial tension when these groups as a whole are in fundamental agreement. For example, a survey of 5,000 students at 40 colleges showed that, at predominantly white colleges, 76 per cent of black students and 93 per cent of white students agreed that all undergraduates should be admitted by meeting the same standards. At predominantly black colleges, more than 95 per cent of the students of both races agreed. This divisive issue inflames campuses across the country because college officials respond to the vocal activists."

In many instances, it is the race-based policies of college administrations, particularly admitting lesser-qualified minority students to fulfill a racial or ethnic quota, which have fueled racial tensions on the campus. Dr. Sowell notes that university officials ". . . wholly ignore the very possibility that the policies and practices of the colleges themselves may have been responsible for the hostile racial climate on campus. A professor at San Jose State University noted among his painful experiences hearing a black woman who 'said she'd never been called a nigger till she got to this campus.' An Hispanic student at Cornell likewise said that she 'had never experienced racism in my face before I came to Ithica.' When 70 per cent of the graduating seniors at Stanford say that racial tensions have *increased* during their time on campus, that does not suggest a 'vestige,' if only because a growing 'vestige' is a contradiction in terms."

Thus, when Dr. Ira M. Heyman, then chancellor at Berkeley, blamed racial hostilities on that campus on "the larger framework of the general mood in the United States," he completely ignored Berkeley's own racial quota policies under his administration. These policies turned away more than 2,000 white and Asian students with straight A averages in one year in order to admit black students who, in large numbers, failed to graduate. In this instance, racial polarization may be a backlash against double standards promoted by the college administration itself.

Many universities have embarked upon a path of encouraging double standards and self-segregation in response to demands from some black spokesmen and groups which have abandoned the older goal of a color-blind society and have, instead, adopted a program of urging proportional representation in everything from college admissions to representation in state legislatures and the Congress. They have adopted, in addition, a policy of isolating black Americans from

5

the larger society, a direct contradiction to the earlier crusade against segregation.

William Sampson, who heads Chicago United, an interracial group of business and civic leaders, argues that the drive for integration is itself a subtle form of racism. "Integration has curious underpinnings," said Sampson, a former professor of sociology at Northwestern University. "To be for integration is to believe that blacks and Hispanics are deprived if we can't be around white folks. That is the essence of racism."

Harold W. Cruse, professor emeritus of Afro-American studies and history at the University of Michigan, states that the civil rights establishment was wrong to promote integration. He declares: "No point in us crusading under that banner. It's not a question of integration being right or wrong. The issue is that sociologically, psychologically, biologically and racially it is not going to happen . . . never mind that we have more integration than 40 years ago, more civil rights. Integration is humanly impossible because groups do not disappear."

In October, 1993 Walter Cronkite hosted a program entitled "The Faltering Dream," which focused on successful black professionals who have chosen to live in black neighborhoods and on black college students who socialize mainly with other blacks on campus. Cronkite stated that, "Many blacks now prefer to be equal but separate."

In Prince Georges, County, Maryland, Cronkite found "affluent self-segregation" complete with comfortable houses, safe streets and a country club. Former Atlanta Mayor Andrew Young sees the voluntary segregation as "a determination to retain your own identity. We want to be what we are." At the University of North Carolina at Chapel Hill, Cronkite found white students who said that they would like more inter-racial mingling and black students who showed little interest.

Columnist Nat Hentoff (WASHINGTON POST, July 10, 1993) described a visit to Roslyn High School on Long Island, New York. At a lunch with editors and reporters for the HILLTOP BEACON, its monthly newspaper, one of the reporters showed him a letter on the op-ed page of a recent issue. A senior, Josh Bloom, had described what happened to him in the hallway next to the gym: "A group of black students refused to let me pass because I am a white male. They insisted that I and all other white males must, in their words 'go around another way.' They did allow females and black students to pass through."

Bloom refused to obey, and as he attempted to go through the blockade, he was pushed several times. In his letter, he emphasized, "The black students of this school should not be allowed to dominate this area." Nat Hentoff notes that, "Bloom's main concern was segregation. Black self-segregation that led to the segregation of others. . . .

I asked the reporters and editors of the school paper if any had experienced the same recurring problem. Most had. . . . Later in the day, I asked a teacher who had been in the school for many years why nothing had been done to remove the blockade. It's not only a source of continual frustration and even humiliation for many students, I said, but the attitude of those particular black students breeds stereotypes, racist stereotypes. 'You have to pull all of this in context,' she answered. 'There are about 60 black students out of 700 here. We want to keep them in school. They're disadvantaged. Some of them need more attention than most of the white students. That's why we don't come down hard on them for blocking that corridor.' I pointed out that this attitude by presumed educators could confirm in the minds of some black students that they are constant victims requiring special treatment. It seemed a rather bizarre way to enable them to have authentic self-esteem for the journey through the rest of their lives."

Ironically, just as the larger American society seeks to fulfill the traditional goals of civil rights advocates and move toward a genuinely color-blind standard, it is many black Americans who are moving back toward segregation. Demographer Reynolds Farley and colleagues at the University of Michigan's Population Studies Center recently compared residential preferences of blacks and whites as revealed in two large surveys, one in 1976 and the other in 1992. They found that whites in Detroit had grown slightly more comfortable about black neighbors while blacks have been backing away from white neighborhoods.

In 1969, black civil rights activist Bayard Rustin, observing the growth of demands for special black studies departments at colleges, warned that, "Black studies must not be used for the purpose of image-building and to enable black students to escape the challenges of the university by setting up a program of 'soul courses' that they can just play with and pass." That same year, NAACP Executive Director Roy Wilkins condemned the creation of "sealed-off black studies centers" for "racial breast-beating."

The lowering of standards for the hiring of black faculty members and the admission of black students in pursuit of affirmative action policies has led directly to the expansion of such African-American programs. A Carnegie Foundation study by David Reisman found "non-scholarly black faculty members who seek to maintain their precarious hold on academic life by building up a cadre of militant followers, threatening to charge the institutions with racism if it releases them."

In Thomas Sowell's view, these tendencies fuel the campus push for self-segregation: "Minority faculty hired preferentially face exactly the same problem of self-respect as the students admitted under double standards. It is fundamentally the same mismatching situation . . . In these circumstances, for mismatched minority faculty to accept the intellectual standards around them and the scholarly thrust of their colleagues means losing their own self-respect. But to denounce the standards they do not meet, and decry as 'irrelevant' the scholarship they cannot match, at least enables them to hold their heads up and to achieve some recognition as a force on campus. However, to maintain even this tenuous respectability requires that they have behind them the support and implied threat of minority students—which in turn requires that they promote among those students not only a sense of separatism but also of paranoia, a sense that white professors are out to 'get' minority students, that low grades are symptoms of repressive racism, etc."

Many years ago, Dr. Kenneth Clark, the black psychologist whose research demonstrated the damage done to black students by segregation, expressed concern that many well-meaning white educators might inflict serious damage by treating black students to a standard different from that used for white students. He said that, "A lot of harm is done to black children by certain kinds of compassionate teachers and administrators. They try to make it easy for black kids. They hold them to lower standards. But by not demanding more of them, they don't enable them to learn their potential."

Today, Dr. Clark argues that black critics of integration "are misguided, wrong and terribly sad people." He states that, "I think segregation of any kind is racist and I am against racism whether you say you like it or not. Segregation is damaging to the individual, damaging to the society's claim to justice and damaging to whites as well as blacks. . . . What they are telling me is that they have been segregated and part of the damage done to them is that they have feelings of inadequacy. They don't want to compete. They feel inferior."

Michael Meyers, head of the New York Civil Rights Coalition, believes that the support for segregation among some black Americans is not a serious position but "a fashion, a fashion of racial separatism."

When Meyers was a student at Antioch College he protested the administration's creation of an all-black dormitory and study center. Kenneth Clark, then an Antioch trustee, supported Meyers. For taking this position, Meyers was beaten up by some black students and Dr. Clark resigned from the Antioch board in protest. Meyers proceeded to file a complaint against Antioch with the Department of Health, Education and Welfare. The college said that the segregated building was a "theme dorm," as colleges today argue with regard to their own segregated facilities. Meyers said that he saw nothing new in Antioch's variation on the theme of segregation. Meyers won the case. Today, however, segregation seems to have gained a strange new respectability.

Meyers now laments that, "Everyone has slipped into talking about segregation as the practical and pragmatic thing to do because it is the easy thing to do. More and more people really do believe that skin color determines personality, culture and even intelligence. The racialists among civil rights activists have propagated that myth. It's the same myth put out by the white segregationists, but the black segregationists have forgotten that. They have no idea of the history and invidious use of segregation so they are all kowtowing to the segregationist line as practical."

A former assistant director of the NAACP, Meyers points to the irony of seeing that organization in the forefront of opposing interracial adoptions: "They'd rather have a black child in a foster home or orphanage than with a white family because they now believe in race . . . Can you believe that!" Meyers is also sharply critical of the Afrocentric education movement which, in his view, offers an escape to those who fear that they cannot compete in the mainstream American society.

Discussing the dangers of the trend toward self-segregation on the part of many in the black community, Juan Williams, writing in THE WASHINGTON POST (Jan. 16, 1994), states that, ". . . taking care of black children includes providing them with a place in an increasingly multicultural and competitive America. That means encouraging black children to believe in their abilities, to dare to get into the mainstream and compete as equals. Those who see integration as passé unwittingly leave open the door of racial separatism. . . . encouraging black separatism is an extremely high-risk strategy. By providing a convenient rationale for those whites who, statistics show, are already aggressively pushing away from blacks, it is almost sure to weaken the larger society's efforts to allow disadvantaged black people to escape the islands of violence, bad schools and unemployment on which they are now stranded. As I look back on my own life, and that of Martin Luther King, I can't help but conclude that integration—no matter how difficult to pursue, no matter how frustratingly slow to achieve—is far better than voluntary segregation, an idea that the very worst racists would be all too happy to live with."

Unfortunately, the demands for self-segregation made by some black spokesmen are being accepted and acted upon by many within the educational establishment. Shelby Steele, professor of English at San José University and author of *The Content of Our Character: A New Vision On Race In America*, points out that, "The marriage of race and power, the politics of difference, and grievance identities—these are nurtured by the American educational establishment. . . . Those with grievance identities demand separate buildings, classrooms, offices, clerical staff—even separate Xerox machines. They all want to be segregated

9

universities within universities. They want their own space—their sovereign territory. Metaphorically, and sometimes literally, they insist that not only the university but society at large must pay tribute to their sovereignty . . . As a black, I am said to 'deserve' this or that special entitlement. No longer is it enough just to have the right to attend a college or university on an equal basis with others or to be treated like anyone else. Schools must set aside special money and special academic departments for me, based on my grievance. Some campuses now have segregated dorms for black students who demand to live together with people of their 'own kind.' Students have lobbied for separate black student unions, black yearbooks, black Homecoming dances, black graduation ceremonies—again, all so that they can be comfortable with their 'own kind.' "

One representative study at the University of Michigan indicates that 70 per cent of the school's black undergraduates have never had a white acquaintance. Yet, Professor Steele declares, ". . . across the country, colleges and universities like Michigan readily and even eagerly continue to encourage more segregation by granting the demands of every vocal grievance identity. . . . Black students have the lowest grade point average of any student group. If whites were not so preoccupied with escaping their own guilt, they would see that the real problem is not racism; it is that black students are failing in tragic numbers . . . college and university administrators blindly grant black students extra entitlements, from dorms to yearbooks, and build an entire machinery of segregation on campus, while ignoring the fact that 72 per cent of black American college students are dropping out . . . They don't need separate dorms and yearbooks. They need basic academic skills. But instead they are taught that extra entitlements are their due and that the greatest power of all is the power that comes to them as victims. . . ."

The danger inherent in the tendency toward self-segregation must be addressed, not only within the black community but in the larger American society, and particularly at our institutions of higher learning. The Balkanization of the American society into a host of racial, religious, and ethnic groups vying for power and privilege can destroy the common American identity which generations of men and women of goodwill sought and for which many civil rights leaders gave their lives.

The future of all Americans, whatever their race, is tied together in our common nationality. To the extent that we divide our society on the basis of race and ethnicity, we deny each individual the right to be judged on his or her own merit.

Those who now advocate racial quotas, segregated dormitories, and a host of other race-based programs have more in common with a previous age's defenders of segregation than they do with the civil rights movement in whose name they often speak in today's political arena.

Although the confusion and debate within the "modern" civil rights movement—"to integrate" or "to de-segegrate"—was never resolved, only if we return to the vision of a genuinely color-blind philosophy will we be true to the vision of those who fought so valiantly to bring the racial divisions under which all Americans have suffered to an end. For minorities themselves now to seek to rebuild such divisions is to reject completely the vision of those who believed deeply in the American dream and wanted to make that dream a reality for Americans of all races and backgrounds.

Clarence Thomas

CONFRONTING THE FUTURE

Selections
from the Senate
Confirmation
Hearings and
Prior Speeches

Introduction by L. Gordon Crovitz

$8.00 including postage and handling

Available from The Lincoln Institute

Walter Judd: The Living Inspiration

by John Fulton Lewis

It is virtually impossible for me to write an obituary about Walter Henry Judd, born September 25, 1898, in Rising City, Nebraska, within the framework of the traditional newsman's definition of the term 'obit.'

The very word, 'obituary' is derived from early Latin origins in the verb obire (ob – down + ire – to go), about falling, dying, and, later, the Medieval Latin: obituarus—a death report.

Walter Judd never fell down, in the figurative sense, in an entire lifetime of tasks undertaken, and he never let down any person with whom he came in contact, who believed, as did he, in freedom, our inalienable rights or citizen responsibilities. So obituary is just not an appropriate word by any stretch.

Oh yes! Walter Judd did in fact physically leave us February 13, 1994, in his 95th year. That is undeniable. I was among that throng, present and accounted for in either of two memorial services in the vicinity of the capital of the nation he served so well, to acknowledge his passing.

But what all of us shared with his great first lady and bride of life, Miriam Barber Judd (whom he married in 1932) and his three daughters (Mary Lou Carpenter, Carolyn Judd and Eleanor Quinn) and seven grandchildren, was Walter Judd's life remembered and life, eternal—not a death, temporal.

What Dr. Judd was, and will continue to be, was an inspiration to all who knew and admired him, cared for and loved him, worked with him or somehow were touched by him in the course of his life.

Dr. Judd—the man so ably chronicled in Lee Edwards' authorized biography "Missionary for Freedom: The Life and Times of Walter Judd" (Published by Paragon House, New York, 1990, 364 pps.)—served in many capacities.

How do I assess those capacities and prioritize them? Probably somewhat differently than some others might.

I was privileged to research, prepare and produce Dr. Judd's daily radio reports on geopolitics and Cold War tensions for the American Security Council's Washington Report of the Air on 1,100 stations from

13

late 1964 through 1970. I also served as editor of the China Letter for the Committee for a Free China which Dr. Judd founded and headed through much of the 1970s and early '80s.

First and foremost, Walter Judd was the consummate physician, especially if one reads the extended definition of a 'physician' as one who "heals or exerts a healing influence." He was, for so many, a physician to those sick in body, to the sick in spirit or in circumstance, to any in need of his genuine compassion.

Yet in the process of his ministrations to the sick, sound science, good judgment, clear logic and careful medicine governed his decisions and procedures. No matter what the problem, he relied on diagnosis before prescribing and the diagnostics included understanding of the total being or subject to be addressed.

This quality or capacity carried over from medical practice with his patients and from his spiritual practice as a missionary, to his assessments of world and national affairs, of politics, of everyday relationships with people and organizations from the American Medical Association, the YMCA, the Congress of the United States, the American Security Council and scores of others he served, supported or helped to found or manage.

Second, as a missionary sent to bring health and modern medicine to the people of China on behalf of the Congregational Church of his New England forebears, he immersed himself in Chinese culture, history and language.

He thus became the ablest and most effective U.S. spokesman for China, the Chinese people and all Asians who would be free. Of course, it was his futile but valiant effort in the late 1930s to warn Americans that the scrap iron they were selling Japan would not only continue to destroy the lives of the people of China but would someday take a toll of America's youth, that propelled Walter Judd into the national limelight.

Largely at personal expense of limited resources, Dr. Judd toured the length and breadth of the U.S. to make 1,400 speeches over a thirty month period before Pearl Harbor tragically proved him right.

Like so many 19th and early 20th century China missionaries from the West, it is fair to say that Walter Judd was truly devoted to the people of that most ancient civilization.

However, such appreciation for the Chinese was without any sacrifice or compromise of Dr. Judd's fundamental belief and pride in America and the U.S.A.'s superior attributes in government and justice, and our Constitution's respect for the individual's freedom and rights.

These qualities were largely absent in the Asian experience until

3,000 years of imperial, dynastic rule was overthrown and the Republic of China was established by Sun Yat-sen in 1911 and, subsequently, since republican democracy's development on Taiwan and the offshore islands.

Third among the priorities of assessing Walter Judd, I would list the great and common decency of the man. For instance, he never attacked personalities when criticizing the politics and policies of others. He might privately express distaste for or disappointment in some figure in public life or even within his own circle of friends and acquaintances whom we both knew. But not a word of identification would be uttered to the audiences we reached by broadcast or by print.

He was entirely dedicated to accuracy and in the nearly 15 years of my own association with him in the preparation of scripts, articles and newsletters, we established an almost immaculate record—thanks to his repeated insistence and careful scrutiny plus my own basic desire—of not having embarrassing errors crop up in what we said or wrote.

He held very strong convictions and seemed unwavering in holding to opinions to which, before reaching them, he had given much serious thought. Yet, Dr. Judd had an enormous sense of humility when confronted with the possibility that his judgment might be less than fair.

He recognized and often volunteered possible shortcomings in himself which were not apparent to others but he never did this in a contrived, self-deprecating manner. Rather, it was more in the spirit of a confession in confidence—something he sensed from deep within his own heart and mind.

Fourth—and, for this estimation of the man, finally—Walter Judd was generous to a fault, distributing up to half his annual income to causes and charities in which he had strong belief. He was also unstinting in granting precious hours of his time to helping others accomplish projects in which he had more than peripheral intere

I often had the impression that his personal dedication of time and resources after leaving Congress in 1962 was, in part, to assuage his own intense disagreement and disgust with the Congressional pension system.

As a founder of the association of retired Members of Congress, Dr. Judd often expressed the hope that more of them would agree to help him lobby for a curtailment of Congressional excesses—the very excesses which now have become obscene to many observers of the behavior of elected lawmakers: escalating staffs; enormously inflated expense allowances; self-voted pay increases; rising cost-of-living pensions; and, so many other 'perks' unavailable and unattainable for the American body politic.

Lincoln Review

So what is the most important legacy of Walter Henry Judd of Rising City, Nebraska, son of a relatively unschooled, onetime farmer and eventually, a modestly successful lumber yard operator?

Was it his work as a medical missionary to China? As a 10-term Republican Congressman from Minnesota? As a respected statesman who counselled so many heads of state at home and abroad, from Dwight Eisenhower to the Dalai Lama, from Chiang Kai-shek to Lyndon Baines Johnson? As a renowned speaker who reached out to America's youth, on the lecture circuit, to try to explain the growing complexities of a confusing world?

Those and many other things are certainly important but to one who was so deeply and intimately influenced by Dr. Walter H. Judd, the most valuable of his many legacies to all was the legacy of integrity: integrity in personal life; integrity in politics; integrity in medical science; integrity in his mission for his church in China; integrity throughout his life for all that he upheld.

That is why Walter Judd lives. That is why his story can have no obituary in the traditional sense of the word. What he stood for remains, eternally, tall, undiminished and very much alive.

Remembering Walter H. Judd

O n February 13, 1994, Walter H. Judd—M.D., brilliant speaker and renowned lawmaker—passed away at a retirement home in Mitchellville, Maryland, at the age of 95.

Until he began worrying over seeming lapses of memory and the often uncertain recognition of old friends during the last decade of life, he sometimes joked about 'sticking around' until he could oversee putting the 20th Century to rest forever.

For those too young to have known about this man, a few words are necessary:

Dr. Judd was one of America's greatest statesmen in the century now nearing its end. He was also an outstanding medical missionary in Central China where he ran a hospital and, often under virtual house/hospital arrest, found his person and his work threatened either by Japanese field commanders or Chinese communist rebels as war engulfed the entire mainland in the 1930s—long before December 7, 1941.

His fame began in the late 1930s when he came back to the States to warn us, in some 1,400 speeches BEFORE Pearl Harbor, to stop selling scrap iron to Japan.

Judd repeatedly predicted that U.S. scrap metal, being sold to Japanese militarists for use in China, might someday be directed against Americans. Had the Roosevelt Administration and the then isolationist American people heeded the warning, the Japanese attack on all Pacific nations, might have been averted.

In 1942, Judd was elected as a Republican Congressman from Minnesota and he became the pioneering advocate of not only the Eisenhower Administration's China policy but what would subsequently become the Food for Peace program, the Alliance for Progress in Latin America and the sharp reduction of ethnic barriers to Asian immigration.

To those who knew and worked with him, one word, above all, described Dr. Walter H. Judd: the word INTEGRITY. Also, he had a powerful trust in the American people. Time after time, he would say that, given the facts, the American people would make the right decisions for their nation and for the world.

By deed and by word, Walter Judd represented true greatness in America and, thus will be sorely missed.

Walter Judd: An Inspiring Patriot and Missionary

by Allan C. Brownfeld

The death of Walter Judd at age 95 has removed from the American scene one of the most important and highly respected figures of the century.

As a medical missionary in China in the years before World War II, as a member of Congress from Minnesota for 20 years and, most important, as a towering figure of moral integrity in an increasingly squalid political landscape, his contribution was both significant and inspiring.

Dr. Judd went to Nanking, China, in 1925 as a medical missionary for the Congregational Board of Foreign Missions and a year later set out on a 12-day river journey to a mission hospital in Shaowu in Fukien Province. He stayed five years before severe malaria forced him to return home. He returned to China in 1933 as a hospital superintendent in Fenchow, where his mission became a haven for many Chinese fleeing the advancing Japanese armies. He remained in the city for five months after it was captured by the Japanese before negotiating his release.

Outraged by the brutality of Japanese aggression, Judd returned to the United States and began a two-year campaign warning of Japan's military expansionism. Before resuming his medical practice in Minneapolis, he spent his savings traveling to 46 states to speak to 1,400 groups.

GAVE EARLY WARNINGS OF JAPANESE AGGRESSION

Before most Americans were aware of what was taking place in Asia, Judd became a very early opponent of Japanese aggression. With great foresight he wrote to a friend on Thanksgiving Day, 1931: "If the Japanese military party gets away with this straight steal in Manchuria—as it appears they almost certainly will—then disarmament is out of the question and we idealists would do well to face the fact squarely. . . . A victory for the Japanese military party means the world,

19

although it does not yet realize it, has chosen the road of force instead of peace. We aren't willing to take the risks of peace. . . ."

While Japan continued its aggression, the United States shipped it virtually all of the essentials for carrying on the war. During his lecture tour across the country between 1938 and 1940, Judd urged the American people not to give Japan the means with which to conquer China and control Asia. In his biography of Dr. Judd, *Missionary of Freedom*, Lee Edwards writes, "Never before or since has any private citizen delivered so many addresses, often six a day, on a single foreign policy issue as Walter Judd did." Judd testified before the U.S. Senate: "If she [Japan] is not checked by non-military measures now, she will have to be checked by military measures later."

When the Japanese bombed Pearl Harbor on Dec. 7, 1941, Judd was engaged in medical practice. Local citizens in Minneapolis persuaded him to run for the U.S. Congress. Old-line politicians scorned him as a "missionary" who had lived in the city for less than two years. But he surprisingly won both the Republican primary and the general election.

In wartime Washington, D.C., Judd was a singular figure. "Rather than resenting Judd's moralistic approach to politics," Edwards notes, "most congressmen admired it; they decided that the House of Representatives was diverse enough to include even a man who put principle before party. They also recognized his first-hand knowledge of far-off places and peoples they had only read about; a physician among lawyers, a missionary among politicians, an internationalist in an isolationist delegation, a man who voted to satisfy his conscience, not his constituents."

Indeed, Judd was named by colleagues in Congress in 1962 as one of the five most admired and influential members. He was nominated for President as a favorite son in 1964 and in 1981 received the Presidential Medal of Freedom from Ronald Reagan.

At that time, President Reagan called him "an articulate spokesman for all those who cherish liberty and a model for all Americans who aspire to serve mankind as physicians, spiritual leaders and statesmen."

Walter Judd fought many worthy battles. One, which was finally successful, was the removal of all racial clauses from U.S. immigration laws. He urged—year after year—that Chinese and other Asians be treated as equals. Finally, in 1952, Congress removed all discrimination from U.S. immigration laws—the first national civil rights legislation since the Civil War.

UNDERSTOOD DANGERS OF CHINESE COMMUNISM

During World War II and later, many Americans were misled into thinking that Mao Tse-tung and the Communists were merely "agrarian reformers" who sought democracy, while the Nationalist government of Chiang Kai-shek was portrayed as "corrupt" and "feudal." From his years in China, Judd understood that the real situation was quite different and he dedicated himself to fight against communism in China.

History, sadly, proved all of Walter Judd's predictions about the horrors of communism to be correct. As Lee Edwards writes, "Most forecasters are delighted with a .500 batting average; Judd batted a thousand with these predictions. Chinese Communists, not agrarian reformers, seized control of China and instituted a ruthless Stalinist regime that eventually took the lives of at least 34 million Chinese. . . . If Chiang and not Mao had prevailed. . . there is good reason to believe that there would have been no Korean War."

Walter Judd's knowledge of communism was first-hand. As early as 1930, while he served in China as a medical missionary, he had seen the Chinese Communists' "utterly ruthless purges and slaughterings of anyone who crossed their will." After their terror campaigns failed, he said, they tried to convince the world that they were "merely downtrodden patriots," seeking to escape Chiang's "tyranny."

With regard to the role of a legislator, Judd believed that "the Founding Fathers expected a member of Congress to vote according to his judgment as to what is best for the nation as a whole. If events proved his judgment on the most important issues have not been sound, then the people will properly replace him."

This writer had the good fortune to know Walter Judd for more than 30 years. Until the age of 90 he continued to write and to lecture. I well remember a day about 15 years ago when he and I were to appear on the same program in Oklahoma City and several of us went to the airport to meet him. He got off a small commuter plane, just having delivered a lecture in the Ozark Mountains and bounded into the airport, with more energy than those many decades younger.

At his funeral, the Rev. Richard C. Halverson, chaplain of the U.S. Senate, described Walter Judd as the most honorable man he had ever known. He told the congregation that at the moment of his passing, Dr. Judd was listening to recording of the hymn, "Precious Lord, Take My Hand."

Walter Judd—a genuine missionary for freedom—was an American original and it is the virtue of our society that it can produce men such as this. His life and his example will continue to be an inspiration to those who recognize that without such men, the future of a free society would be less than hopeful.

RECLAIMING

THE

AMERICAN DREAM

The Role of Private Individuals and Voluntary Associations

Richard C. Cornuelle

With a new introduction by Frank Annunziata
and an afterword by the author

Available from The Lincoln Institute

"Letter From Seychelles"

by Tyler Norman

A thousand miles off the coast of East Africa lies a string of scattered islands called the Seychelles where in 1881 General Charles Gordon arrived from Mauritius to report on the possibility of fortifying a defense post for Britain.

As ever, the French were a plague in the Indian Ocean for the Brits who expected trouble over Madagascar and the Seychelles could be their trump. Mother England would listen to a son like Gordon. His military exploits in China had made him a national hero, earning him the nickname Chinese Gordon, since he and his Ever Victorious Army had crushed the Taipeng Revolution against the Manchu Dynasty, costing thirty million lives over a thirteen year period.

Later, Gordon earned more kudos as a provincial governor in Sudan where he succeeded in mapping the Upper Nile, establishing a line of river stations, ending slavery, and quelling more insurgency. After a visit to the Seychelles lasting several weeks, where surely the warm winds and tropical seas offered sweet rest to his weary bones, Gordon concluded the islands would be too expensive to fortify and even then would never be impregnable.

While in the Seychelles, Gordon sketched out another theory and one for which generations of tourists and travel agents would forever be grateful: that the Seychelles, Praslin in particular, must be the site of the original Garden of Eden. In his manuscript "The Garden of Eden" he describes the theory of continental drift and how the Seychelles could have been a part of a massive continent named Lemuria stretching from Africa to India.

The General, a reputed boozehound, also thought he had found the Tree of Knowledge on Praslin with its indigenous Coco-de-Mer, *Lodoicea maldivica*, the fifty foot high member of the palm family which has a giant nut shaped like the female pelvis. He wrote, "Thus far I think every requirement is fulfilled for deciding that the site of Eden is near Seychelles . . . The Coco-de-Mer is the Tree of Knowledge of good and evil—the original tree used to test Eve—which has a mystic property . . . It is a tree unique among trees—the Prince of Palms—grown naturally only on this little Isle . . . I have already alluded to the temptation of Eve and surely if curiosity could be excited by any tree it would be this . . ."

Gordon also believed the Tree of Life was the breadfruit; the spongy, softball sized green fruit which most islanders eat like potatoes. A few years later a writer named H.W. Estridge snippily pointed out at a dinner party that Eve would not only have had a hard time scaling a giant tree in order to pluck her forbidden fruit, but also must have had a good set of teeth to bite into a forty pound nut with a thick husk. Gordon replied he'd never thought of that. History has not recorded whether or not one barbed comment at a party dashed General Gordon's dream that he had indeed discovered the Garden of Eden.

Memories of the peach and beauty found in these one hundred and fifteen granite and coralline islands must have graced Chinese Gordon's dreams from time to time. We know this because he took the trouble to design a coat of arms where a Biblical serpent wraps around the trunk of a Coco-de-Mer tree, a giant tortoise gazing alongside, and he coined an appropriate motto, "Festina Lente," Hasten Slowly, the words Emperor Augustus offered as counsel to his staff. Gordon's notes do indicate he was completely overcome by the Seychelles so perhaps he planned to return to his Eden one day. Biographers say he intended on retiring to Egypt once he crushed the Sudanese rebellions.

Chinese Gordon never came back to the Seychelles nor did he retire to Egypt. Instead, he returned to Khartoum to evacuate Egyptian forces which for months had been besieged by a band of Sudanese rebels led by a mystic named Muhammad Ahmad, or almahdi. General Gordon's job was to rescue the troops, recapture the garrisons at Berber, Suakin, and Khartoum, and set up a provisional government. With his experience, Gordon was sure he could smash the Mahdi so he never called for fresh troops. The siege of Khartoum lasted ten months and on January 26, 1885 rebels broke through defense lines, overrunning Khartoum. Chinese Gordon was speared to death on the palace steps.

General Gordon was never blessed with another trip to the Seychelles, but I was. After an eleven year absence, I returned this summer to observe the first democratic elections since 1977, the same year France Albert Rene staged a coup and forced a brutal Communist dictatorship on the country. Since April of 1992 he has steered the nation towards democracy and as if to make up for lost time, the

Seychellois have gone to the polls three different times since then. In July of 1992 they elected a constitutional commission; in November they voted down a one-party constitution Rene tried to bulldoze on them; in April, after months of televised debate which everyone watched like a miniseries and made all the participants celebrities, they voted Oui for a referendum legislating a new constitution loosely based on that of the U.S. In July they elected a new president and national assembly.

I had been hired by the Democratic Party, the key opposition to Rene's Seychelles People's Progressive Front (SPPF) to fly down for three months and help edit their party newspaper, *The Seychelles Weekly*, write the Democratic Party manifesto, train journalists (those with the correct politics), and print whatever I could in the international press.

This was not my first trip to General Gordon's paradise. In 1980 I arrived on a sailboat and stayed for two years, leaving in 1982 under tragic circumstances. My Seychellois boyfriend, at the age of twenty-eight, died suddenly from leptospirosis, the infectious disease from the bacteria *Leptospira* picked up from animals and causing jaundice, meningitis, and kidney failure. His name was Francois Hetimier and he had drunk some contaminated *baca*, homemade wine.

A week after the funeral, a hundred odd soldiers mutinied while the President was vacationing in the out islands and although they quickly captured key installations, the leaders paused mid-battle to pick up girlfriends and drinks, neglecting to seize the airport. By the time the beers and nuzzling were finished, Rene, thanks to a close friendship with Julius Nyere, had flown in a jumbo jet full of Tanzanian soldiers clothed in new uniforms, carrying new machine guns. For three days we were under twenty-four hour curfew as the fighting raged in the streets of the capital and dozens of bodies later, I knew my Seychelles sojourn had come to an end. The U.S. Embassy, preparing for an evacuation of all Americans and key components of the tracking station built in 1963, advised me to leave because of the precarious political situation spreading like smoke. I flew home in September of 1982.

Fate has been kinder to me than General Gordon insofar as I have never had to face the spears of the Mahdi, but one ponders what he would think if he could see his Eden today. It is certain there is little left of the Seychelles Gordon cast an eye upon in 1881 other than the sweep of unadulterated beauty found in this archipelago which is home to some of the world's most unique flora and fauna.

Eleven years ago I left an island nation with people of Asian, African, Indian, and European descent who were still carefree in spite of Rene's harsh Marxist-Leninist state. The Seychellois were warm spirited and generous, terrible employees and good liars, deeply superstitious and faithful to their *gri gri* magic while practicing Catholicism. Entertain-

25

ments were listening to radio shows from the BBC since there was no television; drinking toddy (palm wine tapped from the coconut tree); making love; playing dominos; dancing to the popular music *sega*, similar to Caribbean calypso, or *moutya*, an African dance where people jump up and down slowly to drumbeats; an occasional trip to the cinema or soccer match; family barbecues; gossipfests on porches; and wakes where tears were shed quickly and then attention centered on the drinks being served and the gunny sacks laid down outside where everyone (except the bereaved) played cards and gambled by candle-light.

Back then, the Seychelles was still a vacationland, clean and ashimmer in the sun and crowded with tourists. Food was cheap and plentiful, crime was minimal, banks were filled with foreign exchange, and aid was still pouring in from the West and Communist block since almost everyone in the world had glanced at the map and realized the Seychelles had a strategic location to African commerce routes and Arabian oil fields. President Albert Rene had been in power for five years since toppling James Mancham. Though he was an avowed Marxist, the country was still enjoying the vestiges of its days as an English colony with a thriving open market economy.

In 1982, to the naked eye, the good life was still attainable in the Seychelles, but there was grit in the glance. President Rene's socialist revolution was putting a vice grip on the islands with a complete suppression of civil rights; mysterious deaths for the politically incorrect; nationalized businesses; expropriated land handed out as favors to key cronies; military brigades for youngsters; and national youth service camps for teenagers where Marxist doctrine and collective farming took precedence over the three 'rs. While the Seychellois struggled with a decline in their standard of living, houses for newly rich politicians, businessmen, and one very wealthy president were built on Mahe.

A lot had changed between September 1982 and June 1993. I returned to a country whose majesty had hardly diminished in spite of more pollution, construction, expansion, and seven thousand extra Seychellois. But over the years the West had punctured Creole living with urbanization. Radios had been turned off because most families, as long as they paid for the yearly $50 licenses, had televisions. Evenings were now spent in front of shows like "The Golden Girls" and "Tropical Heat" or films fetched from neighborhood video rental shops for VCRs. Women no longer cooked on fires and washed clothes in basins or rivers. Most had electricity, even those in the smallest hillside shacks, so there were washing machines, stoves, rice cookers, electric kettles. Mothers, wives, sisters, and daughters were going to need the appliances anyway; the majority now worked because the cost of living was exorbitant, three times that of the United States.

Tastes had changed as well. Few Seychellois still had nets above their houses to catch fruit bats for their curries. Pizza and spaghetti were popular and Coca Cola and Sprite had arrived. So had Nike. Rap music jangled from Radio Seychelles. Rastafarians cruised the beaches. Karaoke was popular in the bars. I was relieved that neither McDonald's nor Kentucky Fried chicken had staked their claim on the Seychellois palate. For the time being.

But along with the considerable list of conveniences and penchant for fast food, the problems we battle in the rest of the world had appeared as well. Sixteen years of socialism had desiccated the economy with annual growth having shrunk from 15% to 3%. Rene's state was carrying a $154 million external debt, devastating where over 90% of the goods are imported, and each year he was overspending the GNP by at least 6%.

Unemployment was rising, especially among the young, and crime soared. Break-ins were a plague. Most anyone of means had been burglarized at least three times and the thieves came of all ages. In the village of Beau Vallon, second in size to the capital city Victoria, a gang of nine to twelve-year-olds had recently been arrested for breaking into numerous homes. Their older compatriots were more dangerous; most were armed with AK47s which had spilled into the black market from the heavily armed militia and the Malo, a Serbian ship bound for Somalia and loaded with arms which the Seychelles had impounded in March. Within a few months, the vessel's four hundred pounds of ammunition had been stolen, no official explanation given.

There were other problems. Rape and murder, both unheard of when I lived there unless for political reasons, were on the rise and the police, either from fear or laziness, were useless. Calls to 999 for emergencies were sometimes unanswered because the police had no transportation. When a gang of young SPPF thugs attacked some guests at a party for Young Democrats in Anse Royale, the policeman told the caller he couldn't come until he had finished his dinner.

As far as crime in the Seychelles was concerned, I knew immediately that lives had changed when I read the headline in *The Nation* the first week I arrived. "The Michels' Murder. Three Life Sentences for Payet" with a front page article describing how a twenty-seven-year old mechanic named Edward Payet and a colleague named Ralph Bonnelame had been given life imprisonment for the murder of a retired couple whom they'd robbed of $100 and then bludgeoned to death in their home. The murder took place in broad daylight.

Another change in the Seychelles was drugs. Any child would admit they were available for the asking at school. Every day I walked the sandy horseshoe stretch of Beau Vallon Beach, a scene famous with tourists because of the blue gallop of mountains rushing down to the sea and the yellow steeple of St. Roch church saluting in the distance, I smelled pot and could pick out which boys, wearing uniforms of light blue and white checked shirts and tan shorts, were dealing drugs under the waxy leaves of the Takamaka trees along the waterfront.

Personally, I had many mixed emotions about coming back, I knew I would find a different country, but I hadn't expected the veil of sadness which covered the first days of my visit. All of my expatriate friends were gone, as most of the Europeans had left the islands over the years of Rene's socialism, and I spent two sad days looking in vain for one Italian friend whom I'd lost contact with seven years ago, discovering not only had she moved back to Italy, but her Sicilian husband had recently been assassinated in a Mafia-style hit. The years the couple had lived in the Seychelles, he had been in hiding. Six couples I knew were divorced; one fellow was in prison for stealing money from his brother-in-law; and many of the elderly I'd befriended were dead.

My old house in Bel Ombre was closed off by the owner because he refused to rent to Seychellois insomuch as Rene had enacted a tenants rights act giving renters the right to buy after a five year occupancy; the court dockets were crowded with protracted cases of landlords trying to evict squatters. After a few days relaxation, I welcomed the idea of work to distract me from the ghosts.

During the days leading up to the election, I was busy writing the Democratic Party manifesto (done by paraphrasing that of John Major's Conservatives) and editing *The Weekly*. It was obvious the Democrats expected to lose the July 23rd election—pundits knew Rene wasn't ready to give up the presidency quite yet—but all forecasts indicated they would take at least ten out of the twenty-two assembly seats. This would have given the Opposition a stentorian voice which President Rene, the Seychellois, and the international community could take seriously.

By midnight on July 23rd, the Democrats and their supporters knew Albert Rene had hoodwinked them. Not only did he win the Presidential election, but his SPPF took twenty-one out of twenty-two assembly seats (only losing one from sheer bad luck), a striking blow for the Democrats. Now that time has passed and the Party has been able to compare notes and take stock, it has become grossly apparent what a sham the election was.

In spite of the glowing reports from the twelve observers sent by various nations, the only promising point was that unlike last July's election for the constitutional commission, there was minimal violence: one stabbing; a wounding by a detonator from a fishing vessel; a few shops owned by DP candidates or supporters burned; and a lot of street fighting, swearing, boozing, hate mail, crank phone calls, and DP children being chased by young SPPF toughs.

With 86% of the electorate voting, France Albert Rene took 59% of the vote; Sir James 36%, and the smaller opposition party, Opposition Uni, 3%. The devil himself conducts Seychelles politics. The people have been battling a totalitarian regime for numerous long years and the moment multi-party politics wash upon their shores, rather than band together to pull down Rene and his SPPF, some feuded with the Democrats and splintered off with their own parties, later reorganizing under the banner Opposition Uni (known in Creole as *the parti de trois les dents*, the party of three teeth, since their symbol is three circles like those on the Olympic flag).

Throughout the election, the Opposition Uni waged a vendetta against Mancham and not the dictatorship so the Democrats spent most of their time squabbling with Opposition Uni, fending off accusations, and denouncing blackmail with a constant flurry of press conferences and distribution of slanderous Creole pamphlets printed the night before.

One time Opposition Uni did promise to cooperate if DP would hand over half its seats in the assembly, the Democrats replying this was a ridiculous demand. Surely Rene must have chuckled to himself a great deal throughout the campaign since he expected the switch from dictatorship to democracy to be more painful. Unchanged at heart, he had only called for democratic freedom because of the collapsing economy and loss of foreign aid. Let the Opposition snipe at each other like maddened dogs.

The past year in Seychelles politics may have been in the name of democracy, but from the start Albert Rene had a master plan with other intentions. Regardless of the lip service he'd been paying to democracy, he never intended to have free elections. Everything was in favor of the incumbent. President Rene had financial control of the electorate. Over 70% of the population is dependent on the one-party state for houses, jobs, loans, and benefits, and not only did he have the facilities and coffers of an entire nation at his disposal in order to mount a campaign and determine the results, he had many years experience.

The Opposition leaders, namely DP, were all exiles and struggling to win an election based on volunteer efforts and grassroots funding. In spite of Rene giving each party $40,000 a month from the electoral budget to wage their campaigns against him, the Democrats didn't even have a xerox machine until a week before the election and three days afterwards, they ran out of toner. Typically Third World, there was no more available on the island at such short notice.

It was the results of the assembly election which came as a bigger

29

shock to those who had opposed Rene and his SPPF. With twenty-two electoral areas, Seychelles People's Progressive Front took twenty-seven out of thirty-three seats which translates to twenty-one out of twenty-two constituencies; the difference stemming from seats being rewarded on a proportional basis for voter percentages, the first 9% of votes giving a seat, followed by 10%. The Democrats had counted on eight to ten seats yet in the end only received the five proportional plus their one victory seat and Opposition Uni was given one; three solid DP areas were lost in close races to SPPF because of the swing vote taken by Opposition Uni.

In the national assembly election the only seat the Democrats won was my old neighborhood Bel Ombre, a village which so loathes Rene they refused to be bought off by the SPPF which had spent months bribing residents with money, housing materials, and athletic clothes. Because of the amount of money spent, Rene was so surprised he had lost Bel Ombre he had the ballots counted four times. Although the area is only a fifteen minute drive from Victoria, the President rarely visits because his fleet of cars, crammed with bodyguards, is usually greeted with clouds of swear words and shaking fists and children have been known to pelt his speeding Land Rover with rocks. The animosity for the President in Bel Ombre goes back to his salad days with the radical Seychelles People's United Party, and the locals, a mix of all colors and incomes, have always been staunch followers of Queen Elizabeth and Sir James, never wanting the independence Britain granted in 1976.

For them, the last nail in the coffin of Rene's reputation was the night of the coup in 1977 when one of the people killed was a popular Bel Ombre politician named Davidson Chang-Him who tried to stop Rene's grab for power. (A bullet to the head ended Chang-Him's bravery.) It is with befitting political irony that Chang-Him's young daughter Dorothy is employed today as a secretary for the Democratic Party and hoping to make politics a career. She has been key in organizing groups of Young Democrats.

How much does a Third World election like the one in the Seychelles cost? Lots. First, the incumbents have government checkbooks in their pant's pockets and can cut checks from various sources like the National Workers Union (the Seychelles's only union towards which each worker is required to pay a portion of his paycheck even if he's not a member) or the Social Security Fund, the government's biggest cash cow since the SPPF state replaced income tax with this in 1989, hitherto causing IMF to end all aid. Coupled with the availability of money were the use of civil servants; manipulation of the press with the newspaper *The Nation* and the country's only TV station on Seychelles Broadcasting

Company; and all government property from printing presses to office space to cars, trucks, and airplanes.

What most Seychellois realize now, at least the ones who are willing to admit the truth, is that Albert Rene's path from dictator to democratic president was scripted long before James Mancham arrived at the airport in 1992 after years in lonely Putney exile. Four months before Mancham returned to the islands, Rene quickly built district councils in each of the electoral districts on Mahe. The function of these councils, which are run by paid chairman and committeemen, is to 1) extend housing loans from the Seychelles Housing Development Company, the only group offering housing loans since there is no local capital market, 2) award social security benefits, 3) cancel loans and benefits for any ingrates, and 4) keep political and personal tabs on everyone in the district via a computer database.

Joseph Stalin would have loved computers because they make spying and blackmail convenient, especially in a nation as small as Seychelles. The one-party state, which until recently maintained a monopoly on computer imports, has been able to conpile a database on every citizen through a national identity card system issued to anyone turning eighteen. This is necessary for jobs, loans, and voting and is denied in cases of political blacklisting. Other means to gather information were the 1989 census, not to mention listening to the often reliable Radio Bamboo, the Creole version of grapevine. It was this data on a family's income, debts, political affinities, and dirty linen which gave the district council its leverage, where each committeeman was assigned twenty households per district as his bailiwick.

To understand the power amassed by SPPF over the years through their intimidation tactics, one must remark upon the smallness of a country like this. For all the encroachment of Western life, the Seychelles is still a nation where most have never received a letter in the post. Even today the mailman has to hunt for many residents by word of mouth in order to deliver mail.

Besides the coercion used thanks to the information stored on computers, SPPF also campaigned with a long list of dirty tricks in hand. Most of the electorate, especially the uneducated farmers, fishermen, and laborers, gave away their votes because of lots of gift giving. Among the items handed out indiscreetly and by the truckload were tin roofing, cement, sand, plywood, toilets and pipes.

During the weeks leading up to July 23rd, government ministers were overheard in rural districts promising land and housing loans. Officials were seen paying off small shopkeepers' bills. Other lures were granting social security pensions (running about $200 a month—much money in a country where the average salary is $300 to $400); deferring

31

loan repayments; offering emergency housing to the poor; and paying off members of the Seychelles People's Defense Forces with raises and bonuses, not to mention giving millions of rupees to army headquarters at Bel Eau.

What did the Seychellois think of Albert Rene and SPPF's idea of campaigning? Firstly, they only heard the stories while sitting on their verandas or gossiping at the marketplace because Rene slapped a blackout on all election news during the days leading up to the 23rd. The only footage we saw concerning the government besides the likes of films on giant tortoises and orchid production were clips from the national p.r. program of building footpaths and fish markets, extending electric lines, purchasing fifty-two new buses (actually second hand from India), and repairing roads.

As previously, the government work programs stopped shortly after the election. Roads either go nowhere or stay unfinished. Lastly, the greatest event in the government's effort to spruce up its tarnished image was hosting the Indian Ocean Games in August. This was the Seychelles biggest sporting event ever, where five neighboring countries competed in a dizzying array of events in facilities costing the country $20 million (government statistic and therefore jimmied) and will probably never be used again on a productive basis because they are too large.

As for personal integrity and how two thirds of the electorate could have been bought for so little, it is a fact the Seychellois by nature are very materialistic. They are also poor, albeit poor on a tropical island has a very different connotation from poor in Cabrini Green or Applachia, so they enjoyed the handouts. Many saw no fault in selling their votes for new toilets or bags of cement; sixteen years of austerity has created a nation of self-servers.

The deceit on the part of the SPPF continued the day of the election. Checkpoints were set up all over the main island where government social workers, holding old people's national identity cards which enable them to receive their pensions, pressured individuals to vote SPPF before driving them to the polls. Many elderly were chauffered from district to district voting more than once; there are numerous voting registers showing people having voted twice within a half an hour. There were also reports of many senior citizens pretending to be blind or handicapped in order to qualify for a relative or district council staffer to accompany them inside the voting booth.

Also reported were pollworkers passing ballots marked for the SPPF candidate and President Rene from one voter to the next in the same envelopes. The Democratic Party and Opposition Uni had volunteers in each district, but they were completely outnumbered and the Commonwealth observers seemed more interested in buying souvenirs and filing sunny reports. "We could never have expected Albert Rene to go to bed a dictator and wake up a democratic president," said Rose-Marie Hoareau, DP candidate for English River, a district where SPPF was not only holding senior citizens' social security pensions until election day, but also padded the voting rolls with hundreds of new residents during the months beforehand.

Three days later, France Albert Rene, looking fit and rested, was sworn in as president of the Third Republic of Seychelles to a chorus of congratulations coming from all over the world. His first gesture was to cancel the holiday June 5th, the day of the coup and national liberation day, and by week's end, he had announced his new ministers ("Plus Ca Change, Plus C'est La Meme Chose," said one of the Opposition newspapers,) and the assemblymen were sworn in at a Statehouse ceremony; as the five members of the Democratic Party took their oaths, each held a royal blue *Bible* high in the air as dozens of very unhappy SPPF looked on. Soon after the ceremony, President Rene and Sir James left on extended holidays and for the first time in a year, the Seychellois put politics behind them. Technically, until the national assembly reconvenes October 14th, it's their silly season.

Little is certain in history and politics, but it is assured the Seychelles will never return to the days of deportations, imprisonments, torture, assassinations, disappearances, confiscation of land and businesses, and blacklistings used by Albert Rene and his coterie to insure absolute power.

The world is a different place from that balmy June night in 1977 when he staged his coup; the Soviet Union is gone and Superpowers are no longer preoccupied with the archipelago's strategic location and couldn't afford to sustain their interest anyway. Between the collapse of Communism, the slamming shut of Western pocketbooks, the drain of the welfare state, and the failure of the socialist economy, the President is broke and knows his version of *la revolution* is over. With the eyes of the world watching carefully over his shoulder, now he must answer to a constitution and a parliament where the tiny yet clever Opposition (three of the six trained overseas as lawyers) are much more sophisticated in the ways of parliamentarianism than the SPPF members.

Eavesdrop on conversations today in the cafes of Victoria, and inevitably, the name of Albert Rene is mentioned. Since all aspects of life revolve around him, he is the center of everything, the great determinant.

In spite of his force of victory on July 23rd, observers believe Rene is no longer up to the job of president and is whiling away time until he can step down at his own leisure, saving his skin by cooperating with the Opposition. There well may be truth in this. He has recently moved into a new beach house tucked away in a private part of Mahe called

Anse Polite, discreet, and surrounded by security: a comfortable haven for any retired dictator. Further, for years he has been rumored to be in bad health, often staying in bed because of "influenza," traveling to the Far East from time to time allegedly for blood transfusions.

Recently, although the national press denied all rumors, he reportedly collapsed on the flight he was taking to Singapore for his vacation and for one week the Bamboo Radio crackled with the news he was 1) in France after suffering a massive stroke, 2) in London after suffering a massive heart attack, and 3) dead. President Rene returned to the islands in August to prepare for the opening ceremonies of the Indian Ocean Games and with an air of "Reports of my death have been greatly exaggerated," he admonished his countrymen for spreading such vicious rumors. Despite his denials, many Seychellois believe something is amiss and that he is suffering from some malady.

On a personal note, there has been a change in President Rene's life which has probably colored his view of the future and the importance of holding on to power. He is in love. Last spring he divorced his wife, who was battling cancer at the time, and married his beautiful Bahai mistress with whom he has a baby. Associates of the new First Lady say they don't believe she is as interested in politics as her predecessor and would probably like him to step down and concentrate on family life. Meanwhile, wags say if the British should build a statue to Wallis Warfield Simpson then the Seychellois should definitely build one to Sarah.

Even if President Rene resigns or at least works to promote a more honest version of democracy, one way or another Seychellois are in for a bumpy voyage. The new government is desperately trying to sort out the economy while officials, sent abroad begging, usually return home empty-handed. Shortages are expected and the cost of living ever increases as locals suffer through repeated hikes in water, electricity, phone, and food. Like the good old days, people are again setting fish traps and planting gardens to avoid paying the prices at the markets.

Tourism is the greatest bread and butter yet despite grand government figures stating that industry grew last year by 18% with 98,547 visitors, the facts belie the statistics. Insiders talk of dropping numbers and complaints of high prices and bad service where little money is spent locally because most travelers arrive on package tours. With round trip airfare from London costing $1600, one night in a mediocre hotel, two meals included, costing $300, and dinner for two in a restaurant running $100 minimum, it is understandable why cheap holidays in Mauritius are the Seychelles' constant reality. If there is one thing tourists have discovered, the world is full of tropical islands.

Like many island countries, Seychelles is a land of paradoxes. In the past it struggled with identity as a largely African population lived the lifestyle found in an English colony. Now it contends with the infra-structure of a socialist state under the name of democracy. This Janus will not resolve itself easily, especially since the shadow of Albert Rene still reaches far and wide across these sun flecked beaches and mountains. As for the future, General Gordon's motto for the place he compared to Eden springs to mind. "Festina Lente." Hasten Slowly.

The fairest, simplest, most efficient, **and workable** plan yet proposed

Robert E. Hall
Alvin Rabushka

THE FLAT TAX

HALL-RABUSHKA SIMPLIFIED FLAT-RATE TAX FORM

1985

Individual Wage Tax

Last name

Your social security number

Spouse's social security no

Form 1

Your first name and initial (if joint return, also give spouse's name and initial)

Your occupation ▶

Spouse's occupation ▶

1	
2	
3	

Present home address (Number and street including apartment number or rural route)

City, Town or Post Office, State and ZIP Code

4(a)	
4(b)	
4(c)	
5	
6	
7	
8	
9	
10	
11	
12	

1 Wages and Salary
2 Pensions
3 Total (line 1 plus line 2)
4 Personal allowance
  (a) □ $9000 for married filing jointly
  (b) □ $4500 for single
  (c) □ $8000 for single head of household
5 Number of dependents, not including spouse
6 Personal allowances for dependents (line 5 multiplied by $1800)
7 Total personal allowances (line 4 plus line 6)
8 Taxable wages (line 3 less line 7, if positive, otherwise zero)
9 Tax (19% of line 8)
10 Tax withheld by employer
   due (line 9 less line 10, if positive)
   (line 10 less line 9, if positive)

$8.00 including
postage and handling

Available from The Lincoln Institute

The Remarkable Legacy of Russell Kirk

The death of Russell Kirk has taken from us the individual who may be most responsible for the emergence of an intellectually vigorous and politically viable conservative movement in the latter part of this century.

For all of those who knew him, Russell Kirk was a gentleman and scholar of the old school, always seeking to understand how men and societies work and interact and to carefully delineate which things are permanent and must be preserved and which are temporal and can, often must, be altered.

The author of more than 30 books and hundreds of essays, reviews and columns, Kirk was a popular lecturer, addressing audiences on more than 500 college campuses. His best known work, *The Conservative Mind*, was published in 1953 and presented the intellectual and historical framework for contemporary American conservatism. It was a best-seller when it appeared and has never been out of print in subsequent years. Speaking at a testimonial dinner in Kirk's honor in Washington in 1981, President Ronald Reagan said: "Dr. Kirk helped renew a generation's interest and knowledge of 'permanent things,' which are the underpinnings and the intellectual infrastructure of the conservative revival of our nation."

To those who argued that it was liberal ideas which defined the American experience, in *The Conservative Mind*, Kirk, through an extensive discussion of Edmund Burke, John Adams, James Fennimore Cooper, Nathaniel Hawthorne, Benjamin Disraeli, Herman Melville, T.S. Eliot and George Santayana, presented readers with a different intellectual and moral tradition, one with deep roots in the past—the Judeo-Christian tradition, the experience of Greece and Rome, the tradition of democratic self-government as it evolved in England from the years of Magna Carta.

It was Kirk's view that our nation, if it is to remain great, must remember and understand the historical roots from which it grew. In a foreword he wrote in 1992 for a new edition of *The Roots of American Order*, he noted that, "Lacking a knowledge of how we arrived where we stand today, lacking that deep love of country which is nurtured by a knowledge of the past, lacking the apprehension that we all take part in a great historical continuity—why, a people so deprived will not dare much, or take long views. With them, creature comforts will be everything; yet, historical consciousness wanting, in the long run they must lose their creature comforts too."

The roots of the American order, Kirk showed, went back to the ancient world—to the Jews and their understanding of a purposeful universe under God's dominion, to the Greeks, with their high regard for the uses of reason, to the stern virtures of Romans such as Cicero, to Christianity, which taught the duties and limitations of man, and the importance of the Transcendent in our lives. The roots of our order, in addition, include the traditions and universities of the medieval world, the Reformation and the response to it, the development of English Common Law, the debates of the 18th century, and the written words of the Declaration of Independence and the Constitution.

The beliefs which motivated the Founding Fathers, Kirk pointed out, were ancient in origin: "From Israel . . . America inherited an understanding of the sanctity of law. Certain root principles of justice exist, arising from the nature which God has conferred upon man; law is a means for realizing those principles, so far as we can. That assumption was in the minds of the men who wrote the Declaration . . . and the Constitution . . . A conviction of man's sinfulness, and of the need for laws to restrain every man's will and appetite, influenced the legislators of the colonies and of the Republic. Thomas Jefferson, rationalist though he was, declared that in matters of political power, one must not trust in the alleged goodness of man, but 'bind him down with the chains of the Constitution.' "

In a recent book, *America's British Culture*, Kirk argued that in four major ways the British experience has shaped the U.S.: language and literature, a body of common law, representative government, and what he called "a body of mores," all of which compose an "ethical heritage."

The fact that the majority of present-day Americans cannot trace their individual ancestry to England bears little relationship to the British nature of American culture. Those who would replace William Shakespeare and John Milton in our schools with contemporary Third World authors in the name of empowering ethnic minorities would, in the end, do these minorities great harm, in Kirk's view, because it would deprive them of the very culture that has created the American society they seek to enter. He wrote: "If we ignore the subtle wisdom of the classical past and the British past, we are left with a thin evanescent culture, a mere film upon the surface of the deep well of the past. Those who refuse to drink of that well may be drowned in it."

It was Kirk's hope to persuade the rising generation to set their faces against "political fanaticism and utopian schemes. . . 'Politics is the art of the possible,' the conservative says; he thinks of political policies as intended to preserve order, justice and freedom. The ideologue, on the contrary, thinks of politics as a revolutionary instrument for transforming society and even transforming human nature. In his march toward Utopia, the ideologue is merciless."

The ideologies which have been so costly in our own time — communism, fascism, Nazism—are, Kirk pointed out, really "inverted religion." But, he declared, "the prudential politician knows that 'Utopia' means 'Nowhere,' and that True religion is a discipline for the soul, not for the state . . . In this 20th century, it has been the body of opinion generally called 'conservative' that has defended the Permanent Things from ideological assault."

Conservatism, to Kirk, "is not a bundle of theories got up by some closet philosopher. On the contrary, the conservative conviction grows out of experience; the experience of the species, of the nation, of the person . . . It is the practical statesman, rather than the visionary recluse, who has maintained a healthy tension between the claims of authority and the claims of freedom."

Not long ago, this writer, who has known Russell Kirk for more than three decades, spent a leisurely lunch with him and his wife Annette, at which time we discussed many of the problems facing our contemporary society. He lamented the fact that the evidence of decadence is all around us—growing crime, increasingly unstable families, failed schools, larger and ever more wasteful government—and is not dissimilar to Greece and Rome in their days of decline. Still, he was not a pessimist, for he took history's long view, as he did in the epilogue to *The Politics of Prudence*, which was recently published. He wrote: "We may remind ourselves that ages of decadence sometimes have been followed by ages of renewal." He urged the young to explore the past, discover the roots of our civilization and work to restore its sensibility. "Time is not a devourer only," he concluded.

Both TIME and NEWSWEEK described Russell Kirk as one of the nation's most influential thinkers. For conservatives, he was indeed the founding father of its modern intellectual configuration. He often quoted an 1843 speech of Orestes Brownson, given at Dartmouth College: "Ask not what your age wants, but what it needs, not what it will reward, but what, without which, it cannot be saved, and that go and do." For 75 years, Russell Kirk did just that.

His body of work is likely to remain alive and well as long as men and women seek freedom and dignity and wish to learn how it is to be achieved and preserved. Russell Kirk has left a legacy from which all of us who treasure the values upon which our civilization is based and which must be preserved if it is not to die will draw upon again and again as we continue in the effort to which he dedicated his life.

—Allan C. Brownfeld

Joshua Lawrence Chamberlain: From Antietam To Appomattox

by Edward C. Smith

More books have been written about the American Civil War than any other war in all of human history. The available titles are well in excess of 60,000 with new material being published every year. The vast majority of the books fall into two categories; battles and biographies. Literally hundreds upon hundreds of books have been written on the Battle of Gettysburg and only Jesus Christ has been written about more than Abraham Lincoln.

Ken Burns' highly acclaimed and award winning PBS series, "The Civil War," was for the war what the broadcasting of Alex Haley's "Roots" was for black history. These two landmark achievements became immediate classics and did much toward helping the nation better understand and appreciate its turbulent past. Although "The Civil War" was excellent in re-acquainting its audience with the heroic exploits of the great commanders of the conflict (Generals Grant, Lee, Sherman, Jackson, Sheridan, Stuart, and others), but, what I enjoyed most about the series was meeting the many ordinary, lesser-known (mostly northern) soldiers who in four years of fierce fighting eventually won the war and thereby saved the Union. The most important of these gallant (but hardly known) patriots that Burns introduced the country to was General Joshua Lawrence Chamberlain, a man whose rare combination of gentlemanly character and soldierly conduct established him as the standard by which all subsequent citizen-soldiers must be measured.

In The Hands of Providence: Joshua Lawrence Chamberlain and the American Civil War by Alice Rains Trulock (396 pages, the University of North Carolina Press, 1992) is an excellent addition to the lengthy list of civil war biographies. The author's writing is exceptionally lucid and

well-paced and her insightful understanding of the most critical elements of war (commitment to cause, combat, and courage) reaffirms
the fact that often women are equally capable of discerning the
distinction between just being a man and being *a man's man*. Joshua
Lawrence Chamberlain, more so than any other soldier on either side,
was an exemplary example of the latter. Throughout the book it is clear
that Ms. Trulock holds a deep affection for her subject and yet she
adroitly avoids surrendering to the seductions of sycophantic hero-
worship. If her book can be compared to a piece of sculpture, then what
she has given us is a full three dimensional portrait of a man and not a
faint figure in *bas relief*.

Chamberlain was born in the small town of Brewer, Maine, on
September 8, 1828. Several of his ancestors, on both sides of his family,
fought in the Revolutionary War and the War of 1812 and although
proud of his family's fighting lineage, he prepared himself to enter the
ministry, not the military. As a youth he struggled to overcome a speech
impediment, stammering, and steadily grew in self-confidence and
molded himself into a well-informed and erudite man who eventually
became an eloquent orator. At Maine's Bowdoin College he taught
courses in religion, rhetoric, and philosophy until the Summer of 1862
when he refused to take a generous two year leave of absence (with pay)
from teaching to travel through Europe and instead entered the Union
Army as a Lt. Colonel in the 20th Maine Infantry Regiment.

His peers considered him to be a talented and tenacious member of
the academic community, but his career as a soldier was far more
impressive than his career as a scholar. For example, as a commander in
the field, he saw action at several of the war's most fiercely fought
battles: Antietam, Fredericksburg, Gettysburg, Spotsylvania, Cold
Harbor, and Petersburg. As a consequence of always being in front of
his men during battle, he was gravely wounded on several occasions. At
one point his injuries were thought to be so severe that Generals Grant
and Meade, fearful that he would soon die, awarded him a battlefield
promotion to the rank of Brigadier General, which is the only recorded
case in the Civil War of such an exalted elevation taking place as the
direct result of bravery in the field.

Ms. Trulock recognizes that the highwater mark of Chamberlain's
life occurred at Little Round Top during the second day of the Battle of
Gettysburg when he commanded his ammunitionless men of the 20th
Maine to fix bayonets and charge head-on into the concentrated
confederate assault on this strategic site. The southern soldiers,
shocked by this highly unorthodox maneuver, fell back in fear and
confusion and many were killed and captured. Like many historians,
the author subscribes to the notion that this single rush of gallantry
essentially won the battle and subsequently the war. She argues con-

vincingly that had Chamberlain been more cautious and less courageous, the confederates would have surely taken Little Round Top and
carried the day. Like her, many other students of Gettysburg deduce
from that single fact that there would then have been no third day of
battle and thus no Pickett's Charge and thus no Union victory. Certainly, this victory (over personal fear and the opposing forces) was the
defining deed in Chamberlain's distinguished military service. Nothing
else could ever compare to it.

Joshua Lawrence Chamberlain was a staunch unionist who had no
doubts why the war had to be waged to its bitter end. He was also an
individual of strong abolitionist sentiments who eagerly embraced the
expansion of the war's aims to go beyond reunification to the destruc-
tion of slavery and the southern social order that sustained it. Indeed,
Chamberlain was a frequent guest in the home of Harriet Beecher
Stowe where the author reveals that she,

"... held 'Saturday Evenings' for a group of friends, mostly young
and including Chamberlain, in her home on Federal Street. The
highlight of these evenings was the hostess reading the newest
installment of her latest work before it was sent to "The National
Era", an abolitionist paper that had been publishing it in serial
form since June 1851. She called it *Uncle Tom's Cabin*, and its
publication as a book in March 1852, before the serialization was
complete, immediately caused a great sensation across the country.
Its depiction of slavery, written in the dramatic and emotional style
popular in mid-19th century America, helped exacerbate the high
feelings above and below the Mason and Dixon's line that led to the
Civil War nearly ten years later."

The heated conversations that ensued after these readings had a lasting
influence on Chamberlain and helped to clarify in his mind that the
war, from the beginning, had to have as its ultimate goal the high moral
mission that would eventually translate Thomas Jefferson's words in
The Declaration of Independence ("That all men are created equal, that
they are endowed by their Creator with certain unalienable Rights, that
among these are Life, Liberty, and the Pursuit of Happiness.") into
meaning equity for all.

To her credit Ms. Trulock also shows us Chamberlain as a devoted
husband to Fannie, his well-bred, well-educated and independently-
spirited wife of 50 years, and we also see him as a sensitive and loving
father, and a loyal and supportive son, brother, and friend. But most
significant of all, she shows Chamberlain as a humble man who is
deeply religious, quietly ambitious, proud of his accomplishments, and
a natural leader of men.

One of the strengths of this book is the manner in which the author uses Chamberlain's own words to describe his character and conduct. In addressing his men on the eve of a major battle he said:

"Comrades, we have now before us a great duty for our country to perform, and who knows but the way in which we acquit ourselves in this perilous undertaking may depend the ultimate success of the preservation of our grand republic. We know that some must fall, it may be any of you or I; but I feel that you will all go in manfully and make such a record as will make all our loyal American people grateful. I can but feel that our action in this crisis is momentous, and who can know but in the providence of God our action today may be the one thing needful to break and destroy this unholy rebellion."

In trying to explain to his distraught parents why he chose to re-enter the fray of battle after recently recovering from nearly death-dealing wounds, he said:

"I owe the Country three years of service. It is a time when every man should stand by his guns. And I am not scared or hurt enough yet to be willing to face the rear, when other men are marching to the front. It is true my incomplete recovery from my wounds would make a more quiet life desirable and when I think of my young and dependent family the whole strength of that motive to make the most of my life comes over me. But there is no promise of life in peace, and no decree of death in war. And I am so confident of the sincerity of my motives that I can trust my own life and welfare of my family in the hands of Providence."

Chamberlain's crowning moment as a soldier and public servant came when General Grant appointed him to be in charge of the surrender ceremony at Appomatox Courthouse on April 12, 1865. Like so many other Union soldiers, Chamberlain greatly admired Robert E. Lee and held his confederate foes in high regard for their heroism and supreme sacrifice in pursuit of their misguided dream of national independence. Thus, he conducted himself, and his troops, with the utmost dignity (and deference to honor) that this most solemn and significant moment in American history demanded. Instead of cheers, there were only the tears of the victorious and the vanquished. After the ceremony was concluded he wrote his reflections on the importance of the occasion:

"Although, as they believed, fatally wrong in striking at the old flag, misreading the deeper meaning and the innermost law of the people's life, blind to the signs of the times in the march of man, they fought as they were taught, true to such ideas as they saw, and put into their cause their best. For us they were fellow-soldiers as well, suffering the fate of arms. We could not look into those brave, bronzed faces, and those battered flags we had met on so many fields where glorious manhood lent a glory to the earth that bore it, and think of the personal hate and mean revenge. Whoever had misled these men, we had not. We had led them back, home."

Interestingly, although Chamberlain's valor was widely recognized and rewarded (mostly by receiving more critical combat assignments from his commanding officers) during his years of service, he was not awarded the Congressional Medal of Honor until 1893, thirty years after he and his men had *made* history on the bloody fields at Gettysburg.

The author's treatment of Chamberlain's long life after the war (he died in 1914, 49 years after Appomatox) is very informative. We see his successes and failures in the areas of politics (he served as Governor of Maine for four consecutive terms), in the field of education (where he served as President of Bowdoin College for 12 years), and in business affairs (where he was reasonably successful in a variety of speculative real estate ventures in Florida).

In a sense it is ironic that the same war that received the lives of nearly 700,000 Americans (the hero's life is always *given*, never taken), should also give to the nation in return such magnificent men as Abraham Lincoln, Frederick Douglass, Robert E. Lee and many others. Beginning with Lincoln's immortal words, "With malice toward none, with charity for all. . . .", they would be the noble ones destined to heal the nation's heart from hurt and hate and bind the country's wounds so that the nation could be made new. To this illustrious list of luminaries must be added the name of Joshua Lawrence Chamberlain.

From its start at Fort Sumter, the Civil War was a tale of two armies, the Army of Northern Virginia vs. the Army of the Potomac, and it was simultaneously a tale of two cities, Richmond vs. Washington, D. C., Washington won the war and with victory came the concentration of federal authority (reducing forever the autonomy of "states rights") and thus the city truly became the nation's capital in substance as well as symbol. Since then Washington has made itself into one vast memorial to the Civil War. The community abounds with relics and remembrances everywhere. Sadly, among all of its many statues and monuments to celebrated soldiers and civilians, there is nothing, absolutely nothing, to commemorate the love of country and devotion to duty so manfully displayed by General Joshua Lawrence Chamberlain. Perhaps in the future this omission will be corrected by a grateful citizenry that discovers how much it owes to the faithful service of this one man for whom there was no compromise in his commitment to keeping the founding fathers' dream alive.

Unfortunately, Ms. Trulock died before her book was "born" and thus she was unable to see the printed word or to read and enjoy the many accolades, like my own, that it has rightfully received. Suffice it to say, her book is a "must read" for all those who seek to better understand why the Civil War remains the single most significant event in all of American history.

The Right To Forget Where You Came From: A Defense

by Jason D. Hill

From time to time one hears the remark hurled against an individual who has managed to make something worthwhile of his life: "He's trying to forget where he came from," or sometimes in the manner of a warning: "When you make it don't forget where you came from."

Such statements are often said against those who manage to make substantial changes in their lives, as well as those who dare to rise above the cultural standards of the day.

Since each person is the owner of his life and since each man ought to be an end in himself, no individual should dictate to any other whether he should or should not remember where he came from. What fairness is there in telling an ambitious young slum dweller who lives with an abusive father, who is harassed daily by hoodlums and who finally makes it through his own relentless efforts that he has no business forgetting where he came from?

We hear stories like this all the time. The individual who survives a harrowing childhood, but retains his optimism and ability to fashion his life in his own constructed image. If an individual's past is so painful or uncomfortable, or if the individual has outgrown his community, should the individual not have the right to forget where he came from?

There are several reasons people could have for not wanting others to forget where they came from. 1) To inculcate the notion that the individual, his life, his goals and his values are inferior to those of the community at large (bear in mind that the community is nothing more than the sum total of individual men and women).

2) To induce a sense of guilt in those who for whatever reason wish to separate themselves from their communities.

3) To make morally questionable their decision to live as individualists.

47

4) To strengthen group solidarity by having everyone honoring the same values, tastes and standards.

5) To milk the person in some way. That is, to be a parasite. The attitude would go something like this: "Okay, so you've gone and left the community which nurtured you, the least that you can do is to give something back."

Giving back, however, implies that one took or borrowed something that did not rightfully belong to one, and that the loan must now be repaid.

The truth of the matter is that the success of many individuals is indiscriminately attributed to the community at large. Too few are interested in scrutinizing the details of the individual's life and seeing exactly who is responsible for what. No, such a task besides being time consuming would be undesirable since it could reveal disquieting truths. Since many actually make careers by acting as the spokesmen for the "community" and in milking the individualist of his dignity and his money, such a method could destroy careers.

The man who renounces his greatness and diminishes the titanic role he played in uplifting himself, who turns over his pocket and with an embarrassed grin declares: "Yeah, I've got to give back. What's mine is yours," is held up as the paradigmatic model of the ideal. In reality, he is being an appeaser who, rather than acknowledge his right to his livelihood, capitulates his independence to sophisticated parasites who clothe their greed in packaged catch phrases.

The security of the tribe is much more important to this type of individual than the fastidious adherence to his somewhat ambivalent convictions. His gut feeling tells him something is wrong, but he has been so programmed by "cultural ideals" that he has lost the capacity to judge for himself why he is afraid to trust his gut feeling. The answer may lie in the fact that he, perhaps, expects the community to offer him a blueprint image bearing an amalgamation of manufactured values and identities. Too afraid of the independent thinking that is required for an authentic individual identity, he accepts the one prescribed by the community. He/she is afraid of being labelled as a "sell out," a betrayer of the community.

An independent thinker would ask: "Sell out to what and to whom?" One cannot betray values one has not pledged allegiance to. The free thinker would say: "An expression and affirmation of my convictions and values are not synonymous with selling out my principles. You mean to harness me by imposing your values on me and hope to coerce my acquiescence by name calling and social ostracism. I will not comply."

Anais Nin wrote that "We cannot live communally, we cannot live in groups unless we bring to them an already evolved human being." (1)

48

To extricate himself from the trappings of communal pressures, the aspiring independent thinker and individualist ought not to burn himself out by trying to make everyone into an evolved human being. This might be beyond his powers. What he can do, however, is to hold himself up-the evolved, autonomous man-as an opulent example for others to see and to emulate if they wish.

There is nothing wrong with helping others and, in fact, deep thinkers have long debated the point that mutual aid to others is necessary for the survival of the species. Besides that, many people would agree that giving to others gives us a deep feeling of gratification. Knowing that we have enhanced the life of another person can be rewarding if we truly value life and the maintenance of life.

To look at the situation as honestly as possible, we ought to recognize the fact that an individual's efforts at realizing his goals can be affected by the environment he comes from. It is no myth that an intelligent individual raised in an affluent community whose parents are able to purchase the best education for him will in many ways find it easier to fulfill his wish of becoming a lawyer than a person of equal intelligence who hails from the slums. But we cannot say that the problems of one individual ought to take precedence over the life of one who might have been more fortunate.

In simple terms, the idea can be reduced to this: "My suffering, my wants, my unfulfilled dreams constitute an automatic right to your help and your life, and the dispersion of this aid ought to be left to my discretion." Those who buy into this way of thinking should be honest about their intentions. What they ought to admit is that theirs is not a philosophy of equality and fairness, but one of favoring the lives of some over others.

This aid or help must be based on the individual's discretion. He must decide when he wants to help and the manner in which he will help. This he does because his decision to help and the manner in which he offers help is based on his values and his priorities. Since values and priorities among people differ, then individuals will help in different ways.

The problem with the "community prison keepers," however, is that they have already decided the precise manner that aid ought to be dispensed. They wish to universalize their method of distribution as if it were some immutable maxim applicable to everyone regardless of personal values. The individual who decides that he will simply hold up his achievement as a light of inspiration for others is accused of being selfish. No, the spokesmen declare, he must give 10% of his earnings, or he must visit the inner city schools 15 times a year. They have totally disregarded the right of the individual to decide exactly how he *feels* like giving of himself, should he decide to at all. Or, as Ralph Waldo

Lincoln Review

Emerson, in his essay "Self Reliance," wrote: "You will always find those who think they know what is your duty better than you know it." (2)

Benevolence cannot be coerced, at least not in a free society. If in thinking about the community we lose sight of the individual, we devalue the concept of the community. Since the community is a composite of individuals, in essence we would have accorded an abstraction (the community) a higher status than that which makes the abstraction possible, (the individual). In attempting to extrapolate a principle we would have lost sight of he/she whose life the principle was designed to enhance: the individual.

One of the more uplifting qualities of the human experience is that a human need not be defined by his most immediate existential circumstances. The individual is a constantly evolving being who has the ability to reshape his world, his character and his ideals according to his inner make-up and his projected visions.

Jesse Jackson often declared proudly during his 1988 Presidential campaign the following excellent statement: "I was born in the slum, but the slum was not born in me." Hence, the slum dweller who feels that his present state bears no resemblance to his fundamental vision of himself and that his present address is merely a temporary lodging has every right to forget where he came from. What he must remember most clearly is not where life delivered him at birth, but where in the universe he will come to occupy.

Anais Nin wrote that:

One is not in bondage to the past which has reshaped our feelings, race inheritance, background. All this can be altered if we have the courage to examine how it formed us. We can alter the chemistry, provided we have the courage to dissect the elements. (3)

The insistence of bondaging man to his community is a retardation of man's capacity to evolve. It hinges on the mistaken premise that man is embalmed, static, non-evolving, that twenty years from now his values and orientation will be in sync with the community. It is a system of thought predicated on the principle of social adaptation instead of individual evolution and adaptation. Many a psychologist would argue that this is a prime reason for many mental problems among individuals in our society.

The glory of individualism is precisely this ability and right of man to define and redefine himself in whatever way he pleases. If you do not like the shape of your nose you may have it cosmetically altered. If you don't like your sex you can change it. If you do not like your mental state and you cannot rectify it on your own there are thousands of psychoanalysts to assist. If you do not like the values your parents raised you by there are dozens of competing ones to still choose from in our semi-free society. In our rapidly advancing scientific world, man is discovering that he has increased mastery over nature, over the given, and that if the *given* is incompatible with what he has evolved into then he can make the appropriate alterations.

For the rational man who is concerned with decisions based on his individual nature we might want to say that the good life consists in values and goals which affirm life but not an affirmation based on sheer whim. The method one adopts ought to be based on careful deliberation. One should ask oneself: "Is this choice or decision central and fundamental to me as opposed to a mere fantasy or whim which I may tire of in two weeks?"

Since initially, by virtue of birth, one's residence in the community is outside of one's choice, as one evolves and grows and changes one ought then to have the right to choose one's community even if this means leaving that first unchosen community. This view, of course, is predicated on the notion that man has the power of volition and the ability to choose.

Those who have a fear of cross communal pollination fail to recognize the intellectual and emotional value this form of interaction has. Consider how boring and intellectually restrictive it would be to associate with only your co-workers or only family members. Cross communal interaction has the potential to universalize the individual by exposing him to the fascinating variables which constitute the rest of the society in which he resides. True, not everyone desires this. But those who do not should refrain from preventing those who are interested in the world beyond their backyards from discovering the wider spheres of the universe.

If one turns to the realm of art and at the raging debate over group proprietorship in relation to the portrayal of "Ethnic Art," one sees the significance of this point. William Styron was heavily criticized for his novel, *The Confessions of Nat Turner*, as he was for another novel, *Sophie's Choice*. The first novel dealt with the only major slave revolt in this country which was spearheaded by the slave, Nat Turner. The second dealt with the traumas faced by a Polish Christian woman during the Holocaust. It was argued that he could not have done justice to a story about a black man because he himself was not black and in the other case many critics stated that in portraying the horrors faced by a non-Jew during the Holocaust he was diminishing the plight of the Jewish people. Similar criticisms might be levelled against a heterosexual who decides to write about gay life, or a Japanese novelist depicting west Indian life and culture.

This community/group proprietorship is still alive today. In the October 1990, issue of *Spin* magazine, American playwright August Wilson states: "Lets make a rule. Blacks don't direct Italian films.

51

Italians don't direct Jewish films. Jews don't direct black American films." (4)

The truth of the matter is that on a journalistic level we can say: "These are the facts-The Russian Revolution occurred in 1917; The American Revolution took place in 1776," and so on. On an artistic level it is an entirely different issue because the meaning of any one event becomes more expansive; its universality transcends the immediacy of facts; its interpretive potential open to a myriad evaluations.

No group or individual has an automatic or inherent monopoly on its truth value. The work may have an objective meaning to its author, but the manner it is experienced by others is entirely subjective and personal. Its potential for the active participation of all (if it is universal as opposed to provincial) makes it a *human*, not *cultural* property. Nadine Gordimer, the 1991 Nobel Prize winner for literature, when asked by *Time* magazine what she thought of the increasing objections voiced by members of specific genders or races who oppose being portrayed by writers outside their groups, said:

> I really appeal to all people and say, if they appreciate literature at all, they should take such imaginative extensions as a gift of insight that writers are trying to pass on to other people. (5)

One might add that this insight is not the exclusive province of writers but of all those individuals who choose to consider themselves part of the universe rather than their tribal villages, those who wish to observe society at large rather than the immediate backdoors or bathroom windows of their neighbor's house.

Sometimes disclaiming one's past enables one to properly redefine oneself. Spared of the pressures of the demand for conformity, leaving the community can give one the freedom to grow and puruse one's interests as one sees fit. The issue of redefining oneself, besides being a corollary of man's capacity to evolve, is necessary when one thinks of the categories our society relegates people into. These categories serve more often to identify a political agenda rather than naming a fundamental and essential characteristic of the group or individuals.

Consider, for example, the names used to identify persons of "mixed blood" during slavery: Mulatto, (offspring of black and white parents); Quadroon (offspring of white and mulatto); and Octoroon, (offspring of quadroon and white, or person of ⅛ black blood). Such labels served no objective racial or physiological criterion. The classifications served political goals. They were the plantocracy's way of devising and maintaining a social caste system. Today, the situation is similar when you consider the many ethnic groups that are lumped under the amorphous term: "Minority."

Author Itabari Njeri writes that,

As most social scientists have acknowledged for years, "race is a pseudo scientific category, constructed to justify the political subordination of nonwhite peoples based on superficial physical differences. There is one race, *Homo sapiens*, and the physical variations that characterize the species do not amount to fundamental qualitative differences as the popular use of the term suggests. (6)

Leaving the community may entail shedding old layers and the concommitant schemas for the world contained therein for new ones, and hence, in this way, one may contribute to the world at large.

Consider the liberal Jew who joins the Islamic faith and imbues his associates with new ideas pertaining to religion and who fosters a new religious order. He may one day go down in history as the man who revolutionized religion. For others he may be the man who left his community. What about the white South African who leaves his country because he is just sick of the injustices of Apartheid and who plays a role in educating people on the irrationality of racist ideologies. For some he may have lost his "racial pride," betrayed his culture. For others he may be a great benefactor of mankind.

Take an individual like Clarence Thomas. His past is well known. Born poor in segregated Georgia he rose to great heights. But today he is accused of betraying his community, forgetting where he came from. He is also a black conservative, which to many, is a contradiction in terms. But what he has done is to blow a hole into the stagnant but comforting view society holds of racial groups, that intellectually and politically the groups are monolithic.

The point here is that one man's example has shaken up the intellectual complacency of an entire nation vis-a-vis its attitude towards the mentality of certain groups. And so one can say that Thomas, by not remaining shackled to the conformist way of thinking that is expected of him, has accorded to blacks the wide variations which make up the human experience, a privilege which is always extended to the majority group.

Thomas and others like himself force us to re-examine the packaged categories we thrust people into because of sheer intellectual laziness. Too often, we are reluctant to admit that the human is really a complex phenomenon, not a lobotomized jock whose essence can be reduced to his conscious philosophical convictions, or the type of music he likes, or the ethnic culture he was born into. Philosopher Robert Nozik writes in *The Examined Life* that:

Once having pigeonholed people and figured out what they are saying, we do not welcome new information that would require us to re-understand and re-classify them and we resent their forcing us to devote fresh energies to this when we have expended more than enough in their direction already. (7)

Thomas must have recognized this idea because in an interview with Dinesh D'Souza in *Diversity: A Critical Journal of Race And Culture*, he speaks about the criticisms and accusations of his detractors. He states: "The problem for my opponents, and for my friends, is that I don't think I fit any of these molds very well. Once people figure this out, maybe they'll leave me alone." (8)

In all the cases outlined, the examples are dramatic, yet the principle remains inherent in every human life: The individual must be left alone to act as an agent of change.

In a truly free society where the present rampant tribalism would be absent and freedom of association respected, one would not need to have any more allegiance to one's community than to tight fitting underwear. In such a case you either lose weight or discard the garment and purchase a new one. And one may do the same with one's community. You may either shrink the scope of your values and individuality when the community bars you from affirming and expressing them, or you may find another one that best affirms your identity.

Immigrants are excellent cases in point. From all parts of the world they leave their homelands for other countries because the degree of their goals and ambitions are disproportionate to the accessibility of opportunities for achieving such goals in their own countries.

The "community prison keepers" ought to bear in mind that the United States of America was founded by individuals who "betrayed" their native communities, who left their homelands to forge new identities. Today, the situation is still the same. Every new foreign engineer, or computer genius or college professor we gain and shower with accolades may be described as a "loss," to some other community, (to borrow the adversary's way of thinking for a moment). Yet, do we subject such individuals to denunciations on the "selfishness" of deserting their communities? No. In fact, throughout history we have at various times actively recruited such individuals with lucrative enticements.

A good dose of introspection and honest, clear thinking will show that in a profound way every human being is both an emigrant and an immigrant; an emigrant who migrates from one state of mind to the next, a state influenced by the constant shifting of values, convictions and emotions. Man's ability to evolve and grow and also to regress makes him a transitory and often precarious emigrant and immigrant within the parameters of his own being. The liberated man only wants to achieve a higher level of autonomy than the tribalist. He wants the perfect marriage between the dictates of his inner life and the concrete occurences of his everyday experiences. Integration and wholeness are his highest aspirations.

Bertrand Rusell states that as long as man's spontaneous activities are such as all the tribe approve and shares in, his initiative is very little curbed by others within the tribe. But,

> As men grow more civilized there comes to be an increasing difference between one man's activities and another's, and a community needs, if it is to prosper, a certain number of individuals who do not wholly conform to the general type. Practically all progress, artistic, moral and intellectual has depended upon such individuals. . . . If a community is to make progress, it needs exceptional individuals whose activities, though useful are not a sort that ought to be general. (9)

In today's clamor for racial and ethnic unity and God knows what other type of unity, this view is treated with contempt and disdain. In our society today if parents were to harness their adult children to the home, telling their forty-eight year old: "You have no right to leave the home you were born into; you were born to serve us; you have a moral obligation to pay us back for bringing you into the world," we would properly dismiss such parents as just plain weird. Yet, when the "community prison keepers" do the same, spitting accusations against those who wish to leave, we beat our tribal drums and melodramatize the war cries, shrieking platitudes and bromides of our own.

It is certain that many will read into this defense their own private agendas, construing the arguments as nothing more than selfish, naive, and unrealistic assertions. This essay, however, is not a clarion call for individuals to leave their communities. It is an unapologetic defense of the moral right of those who wish to leave.

The defense is predicated on the concept of the community as an open and free forum extending goodwill towards its members, not as a slave plantation or prison camp. The defense is made against the backdrop of a culture where race, ethnicity, gender and sexuality are becoming more politicized as the months go by; a culture in which we are not seen first as individuals but as warring tribal factions. Some may rightfully wonder if America has ever really encouraged her citizens to see each other first as individuals. But that, perhaps, will be the subject of another discussion.

Ralph Waldo Emerson seemed to have recognized this type of wholesale drive against the sanctity of the individual for he wrote In *Self Reliance* that

> Society everywhere is in conspiracy against the manhood of everyone of its members. Society is a joint-stock company in which the members agree, for the better securing of his bread to each

shareholder, to surrender the liberty and culture of the eater. The virtue in most respects is comforting. Self-reliance is its aversion. It loves not realities and creators, but names and customs. Whoso would be a man, must be a nonconformist. (10)

This *conspiracy*, however, can end only with a moral battle, when the individual stops apologizing for the fact that he owns his life, that it belongs to him and no one else. The conspiracy will end when the individual finds the courage to liberate himself from the tribe and herd mentality when they run against his deepest values and the basic grain of his personal constitution.

The conspiracy will end only when the individual learns to look within and acknowledge the tremendous untapped power housed in his mind, a power he is often afraid of using because it may result in his standing alone. The conspiracy will end when the individual realizes that it is better to stand alone in splendor than to be companioned with mediocrity and depravity.

REFERENCES

1) *A Woman Speaks: The Lectures, Seminars And Interviews of Anais Nin*. Edited by Evelyn J. Hinz. (Chicago, 1975, 1976 Printing), p. 28

2) Ralph Waldo Emerson, "Self Reliance," in *Individualism: Man in Modern Society*. Edited by Ronald Gross & Paul Osterman. (New York, 1971), p. 32

3) *The Diary Of Anais Nin*, (New York, 1966), p. 126

4) August Wilson quoted in *Spin* magazine, October, 1990

5) Nadine Gordimer quoted *Time* in magazine, October 14, 1991, p. 92.

6) Itabari Njeri quoted in *Emerge* magazine, October 1991, p. 59.

7) Robert Nozik. *The Examined Life: Philosophical Meditations*

8) Clarence Thomas quoted in *Diversity: A Critical Journal of Race And Culture*, October/November, 1991, p. 18

9) Bertrand Russell, "The Role of Individuality," in *Individualism: Man In Modern Society*, p. 4

10) Ralph Waldo Emerson, "Self Reliance," in *Individualism: Man In Modern Society*, p. 30

A Discouraging Hill v. Thomas Anniversary

Tibor R. Machan

A year after the Clarence Thomas nomination hearings it appears that those who wanted Thomas defeated still haven't learned one very important lesson from those events. This is that everyone outside of the principal parties know nothing about who told the truth.

I was glued to the television set or my car radio throughout the hearings. I realized early that the second portion of the hearings would test people's objectivity, more than anything else. I am very interested in how people think, how their minds work, especially when they confront questions to which answers are hard to come by.

In this instance the puzzle was clear from the start: What would members of the Senate Judiciary Committee and the rest of us conclude from having heard an allegation from a respectable person and from some of her friends and colleagues, in the face of the allegation's categorical denial from another respectable person who was given extensive character support from his loyal coworkers and friends.

One would think that by now all self-respecting persons would admit to knowing hardly anything about what happened. Instead, many prominent individuals are demonstrating their failure at elementary logic, the sort of stuff I and my colleagues in philosophy departments throughout the country try to teach our students in basic reasoning courses.

Consider, for example, Professor Ronald Dworkin, one of America's most famous and honored law professors (who holds positions at both New York and Oxford Universities). Here is what he recently said in his New York Times Book Review essays on three books bearing on the Hill v. Thomas affair:

> Anita Hill acted when she did, and maintained her extraordinary dignity throughout, for only one reason that either research or rationality has brought to light. She thought it wrong that someone

who abused power and enjoyed other people's suffering should join a court whose members must rely on their own instincts to interpret the most basic rights of American citizens. She acted out of allegiance not to race or class or sex but only to humanity and the ideals of law.

This is a preposterous bluff—or unbelievable ignorance—from someone who surely cannot be considered naive. Dworkin gave no reason to think he knew more than the rest of us. Indeed, his review essay contained no hint of inside knowledge and new evidence. All he had is wishful thinking and from a prominent scholar and teacher giving vent to such a motivation is simply unforgivable.

Actually, it appears that those who align themselves with either party lack the guts to admit their lack of knowledge. They fail to follow the elementary principle of reasoning, namely, that from ignorance nothing can be concluded. The principle is brought out well in most logic texts—for example, in John B. Bennett's "Rational Thinking" (Nelson-Hall, 1980):

> The appeal to ignorance, or the argumentum ad ignoratiam, is a rather peculiar line of so-called reasoning to adopt. One would think that a rational person, or one who styled himself as rational, would not appeal to the absence of any knowledge whatever to adduce proof of something. But somehow our minds tend to play tricks on us and permit us to set forth conjecture as fact—since no other conjecture or evidence refutes it . . . and assess guilt . . . because the absence of proof seems somehow to substantiate our claim. (p. 44)

If this does not describe the trends of thought evidenced since the hearings, I don't know what would. Both supporters and opponents claim to knowledge that in fact everyone lacks. Dworkin & friends, in particular, keep basing their views on nothing more than conjecture and, perhaps, their personal liking for Professor Hill who was, of course, credible—which means she could be saying what is true. But no one has evidence to prove or corroborate her allegations. Thomas was credible, too. But those who accepted his denial certainly could not claim to know whether he did what Professor Hill claimed he did. They simply trusted him more.

Of course, in a case where a claim is asserted by someone, no one is required to offer a denial until proof is advanced—that is the basis of the judicial policy that one is not guilty until proven otherwise. Dworkin says that this should only hold in a legal context but that is just wrong—unsubstantiated moral charges should be treated the same way. Due process of justice isn't just a legal rule.

Clarence Thomas did not have to say anything at all, given the absence of proof on Professor Hill's part. But when he did deny everything the professor alleged, no one but he could know the truth of his denial. Since no evidence was offered to back up the allegation, clearly no conclusion could be drawn that would contradict him. From ignorance nothing follows!

Too many people, especially members and leaders of various women's organizations, seem, however, to know who was telling the truth—namely, Professor Hill. They keep inviting her to discuss her ordeal and all and sundry matters relating to it, as if it were a proven fact that she was sexually harassed by Clarence Thomas. How come she is treated in this utterly biased fashion? That is the mystery.

Why is there still such unwillingness to simply say "I don't know?" Is there some pressure on some of us to have a firm opinion on everything? Perhaps after watching too much Phil, Oprah and Geraldo, with all their opinion-filled guests, some people get the impression that if they admit to ignorance, they are guilty of some shortcoming.

But the opposite is true. Most of us know only so much, even though we hear about a great deal. We are told a lot by newscasters, commentators, editorialists, pundits, etc. But most of it we have no way of assessing or evaluating firmly enough. We certainly had no knowledge of Professor Hill and the events she claimed occurred to say that she is honest, forthright, courageous, and a hero of American womanhood. This is true even if her motivation for lying is difficult to fathom. That may simply indicate that we lack imagination—certainly a good novelist or psychologist could think of several.

And what about Clarence Thomas? He, too, might have been lying—or telling the truth, for all we know. But saying that "He might be telling the truth" is to admit that we do not know.

It is certainly sad to find so many prominent people in this country jump to so many conclusions without an iota of evidence. But then perhaps this is not such bad news, after all. We may see in it an important reminder: Many of our public persona are really not very special persons, after all. They are a bunch of well dressed and well groomed folks who sound off on much even when they know nothing. So perhaps we ought to be on guard about entrusting them with extensive powers over our lives.

Reprint

Order from The Lincoln Institute
$6.95

Lincoln
Review

SPECIAL EDITION

Articles and Speeches by
Clarence Thomas

Architecture and Academic Achievement

by Edward C. Smith

An architect is the most public of artists and often the buildings that they create are constructed to do much more than shelter some form of human interest or activity. Indeed, a truly "useful" building is one that effectively communicates to its occupants its reason for being. Washington, D. C.'s Union Station, U. S. Supreme Court, Dulles Airport, Air and Space Museum, and National Gallery of Art are all exceptional examples -though imitative of structures in other cities- of the idea that a building must clearly articulate its purpose (through its overall design and decorative detail) and be inspirational at the same time.

Nowhere is the "communicative" role of architecture more notice-able than in the architecture that shelters academic activity, in other words, school buildings. In the area of higher education, many American college campuses are known the world over for their awe-inspiring architectural design: Harvard, Stanford, Yale, the University of Richmond, Vassar, Princeton, and the University of Virginia are only a few that come immediately to mind.

Although there is no scientific way to prove this, I am of the opinion that there is more than a coincidental relationship between architecture and academic achievement. Sociologists have demonstrated, with convincing evidence, that our physical environment (equally as much as our spiritual, intellectual, and emotional environments) can be immensely influential in the formation of our character and conduct.

In Western culture, the medieval universities (the antecedents of our own institutions of higher learning) were born of the will and wisdom of ecclesiastical orders and associations. It was clearly understood that humans are different from animals and although we share with the lower species of life the five senses of sight, sound, taste, touch, and smell, we are, nonetheless, superior in that mankind also has the additional senses (which are totally absent in the animal kingdom) of

61

humor and tragedy; we also possess an intellect and a soul. The theatre became the forum for the expression of comedy and tragedy -and all the joys and dramas of life expressed in between these two extremes- while the churches, synagogues, mosques, temples, and schools became "forums" for the soul and the intellect.

A religious building was expected to be a beautiful manifestation of the mystique and majesty of the faith. No expense was considered too great in the construction of a house of worship and prayer. Since it was mostly religiously-oriented groups that created the early schools in both Europe and America, the same attitude was applied in the creation of academic buildings as well. Centuries ago, Abbot Surger, prelate of the great Abbey of St. Denis in France, who many consider the founder of Gothic architecture, understood intuitively the symbiotic relationship between utility and beauty when he said, "Expense in the pursuit of elegance is not extravagance; it should be expected since all are entitled to it. The dull mind rises to the truth through the contemplation of the beautiful . . . for beauty exists simply and solely to serve, it is God's most enduring, enriching, and democratic institution."

Yale University, founded in 1701, is the nation's third oldest institution of higher education, only Harvard (1636) and William and Mary (1693) predate it. The school's motto, "For God, for Country, for Yale", when it was originally adopted generations ago, was an accurate characterization of the intimate relationship that many scholars sought to establish between prayer, patriotism, and study. To such academics, beginning the school day with prayers, followed by a salute to the national flag, was simple acknowledgement of the proper order of priorities. Today, sadly speaking, such rituals and routines have been almost entirely removed from schools under the guise of respecting and preserving the separation of church and state.

Traditionally, the cultivation of the intellect was conducted with great care and discipline and attention to detail. Teachers were treated with great respect and admiration because their profession was considered an honorable vocation, a noble "calling" to foster the academic formation of others. Therefore, it was expected that in any given community the three most prominent buildings would be the churches, the schools, and those structures designed to house the offices and activities of the civil authorities.

Today, by the standards of test scores, drop-out rates, college admissions, and other such measurements, the public schools in our nation's capital are routinely evaluated as one of the worst systems in the country. Well before his inauguration, President Clinton made it perfectly clear that his only child would attend one of Washington's many prestigious private schools and, in this regard, most members of his administration have chosen to follow his example. Thus, it is difficult for many people to realize that during the twenty year "golden age" era, between 1945 and 1965, the public schools of Washington were considered to be among the very finest in the country. Then, unlike today, the system was heavily populated with the sons and daughters of Congressmen, diplomats, bankers, doctors, lawyers, and numerous other professionals. In fact, there was such a high degree of achievement and community pride in the schools that, by and large, those families who chose to enroll their children in private schools or parochial schools were making a social or spiritual statement, not an educational one. When the black and white schools of Washington were consolidated in 1955 (as a consequence of the *Bolling vs. Sharpe* court decision) it brought together two formerly separate but equally superior systems of instruction.

The conditions that caused the sudden collapse of this glorious era are many and multi-faceted. However, among the most significant was the court-ordered removal of the "track (ability grouping) system" in 1967, the immediate consequence of the *Hobson vs. Hansen* decision, which fueled the flight of the black and white middle class from the city to the suburbs, a migration made all the more attractive with the opening of the Capital Beltway in 1965, and the passing of the federal Fair Housing Act in 1968 which made the nearby suburbs of Maryland and Virginia both accessible and affordable to middle class blacks. Today, an enormously large number of the professionally employed blacks who currently reside in the suburbs, especially in Prince Georges County, Md., have their roots in Washington, D. C.

Most of those middle class residents who chose to remain in the city simply withdrew their children from the public schools and enrolled them in the in-city private and parochial schools.

In the glory days of the "golden age" students attended classes in buildings of outstanding architectural ambiance, most of which were designed in the classical-Georgian architectural style which is so prominently present on the campus of the University of Virginia. Interestingly, while serving as President of the United States, Thomas Jefferson, the founder of the University of Virginia, also served as the first President of the Board of Trustees of the D.C. Public Schools from 1805 to 1809. Thus, architecturally speaking, one can easily surmise that Washington's earliest school's aesthetic appearances helped to serve as a visual link to Jefferson's vision of the role of public education in a democratic society.

The city's population grew enormously during the periods between World Wars I and II and thus there was a great demand for additional school construction. Such school buildings as Western High School (now the Duke Ellington School for the Arts), McKinley Technical High School, Eastern High School, Jefferson Jr. High School, Lafayette Elementary School, and the Sumner School (now a city museum and archives of local public school history) represent a small sampling of the many magnificent public school buildings that adorn Washington. Their structural elegance eloquently stated to pupils, parents, and teachers that the education and preparation of youth was a very important matter and was best accomplished in a serious setting that evokes contemplation and commitment to achieving academic excellence. To reinforce this sentiment, teachers and administrators generally attended school dressed in their "Sunday best" and most students did the same. Like its multitude of monuments and memorials, the beauty of these buildings left a lasting impression on the city's many visitors.

As I remember it, 33 years after my graduation from Western High School, the curriculum was traditional and comprehensive and inclusive of multi-cultural issues. No black student, like myself, was denied learning about his or her past and our race's many contributions to American history and culture. After all, "Negro History Week" (now Black History Month) was founded in Washington, D. C. in 1926 by historian and Educator Carter G. Woodson, who resided in the Shaw neighborhood, named in honor of Colonel Robert Gould Shaw, the Civil War hero from Boston popularized in the award winning movie, "Glory".

Although the Sumner School, designed by renowned architect, Adolph Cluss, has been handsomely restored to its former luster (when it opened in 1872 as the first permanent black school in the District of Columbia and in 1877 when it became the first school in the nation to graduate a black high school class), unfortunately, the academic and architectural capstone of Washington's public education, Dunbar High School, no longer remains. This beautiful tudor-styled building (which undoubtedly was the envy of many college campuses) was torn down in 1976 and replaced (sadly in the same location) by a modern structure of contemporary design reflective of the pure, abstract formalistic functionalism that is so noticeable in the construction of shopping malls and multi-purpose office complexes. Dunbar was widely recognized throughout the nation as the "Phillips-Exeter of black education" and many of its illustrious graduates, which include Benjamin O. Davis, the nation's first black general, Edward Brooke, U. S. Senator from Mass., Charles Drew, founder of the Red Cross blood bank, among others of equal accomplishment, went on to distinguish themselves in nearly every imaginable field of endeavor and bring pride to their school and community.

In this earlier era, schools enjoyed the whole-hearted support of their constituent households and did not have to compete with the electronic media for interest and attention of their students. Today, the salacious and violent offerings of television (especially cable programming), movies, and music are all powerful attractions to young people making it all the more difficult to educate those who have become addicted to perpetual entertainment. It is virtually impossible for educators to do their work well in a licentious cultural environment where the purveyors of hedonistic nihilism are free to aggressively subvert educators' finest efforts and where many parents and civic leaders are only casually interested in the education of their children.

Although most of Washington's beautiful public school buildings still stand, and many are occupied with some devoted teachers, disciplined and hard-working students, and sensitive and supportive administrators, nontheless, they serve mostly as relics and reminders of a bygone era when the pursuit and attainment of a good education was a most sought after and coveted honor. As a third generation Washingtonian and a proud product of the city's public schools, each time I visit the neighborhoods that house my alma maters, I often ask, "Can we ever bring back the past?"

Order your copy
only $5.00

Lincoln Review

THE LINCOLN INSTITUTE
FOR RESEARCH AND EDUCATION

Labor Policy, Minorities and Youth.

The President Vs. The Presidency

by Edward C. Smith

Before reaching the mid-point of his first year in office, President Clinton appointed long-time Republican Party political strategist David Gergen to become a member of his senior level of advisors. Such a drastic decision was an admission of his need to add seasoned veterans to his White House staff of Washington "rookies" in order to bring much needed structure and focus to his administration.

Mr. Gergen is considered by many respected observers to be highly skilled in the amorphous craft of formulating and articulating various public policy agendas and should -if listened to over the long haul-serve the president well. However, thus far many of the problems associated with the Clinton presidency can just as easily be attributed to the nature of the office itself as much as to the mercurial management style of its current occupant.

Our nation's founding fathers, men who waged and won a war that emancipated the colonies from the restrictions of royal rule, wanted to make certain that our republican form of democracy's chief executive would never serve as an elected king. Thus, in their rejection of monarchy, a "triarchy" of three separate branches of government was established. In this rather unique arrangement, the presidency was accorded certain "powers," among which are: to serve as commander-in-chief of the U.S. armed forces and to nominate justices to the Supreme Court (and federal judges to lower courts), ambassadors to foreign countries, and to nominate officials to administer the various departments and agencies of the executive branch of government. Of course, only Congress can declare war and all presidential nominations can be easily rejected by the Senate during the searching (and often wrenching) confirmation process. This can become an excruciating and embarrassing experience, particularly whenever partisan politics are allowed to determine the directions and demeanor of the debate, as was so evident during the Robert Bork and Clarence Thomas Supreme Court nomination hearings.

The president's most significant additional powers are those relating

Lincoln Review

to recommending legislation to Congress, issuing executive orders, making treaties with other nations, and invoking the power to pardon. For his willingness to bear these many, heavy burdens, the president is provided with certain "majesterial" perquisites: the White House as a palatial home and workplace, a "praetorian guard" of secret service protection, transportation by luxurious limousines, customized helicopters, and Air Force One, Camp David as a weekend and vacation retreat, and several other special privileges reserved solely for him and his guests. If not careful, the president can easily allow such comforts and conveniences to "enthrone" him and thereby further distance the man from the daily experiences of the ordinary masses.

The principle problem of the presidency is that the president presides over a White House staff and a council of cabinet officers, absent of any peers. In other words he has no equals in his administration. Every member of his immediate supporting staff and far beyond

into the highest ranks of his appointees in the executive branch, all work for *him* and serve the American people at *his* pleasure, and can therefore be instantly removed from office by *him* through *his* simple request for their resignation.

During 1977 and 1978, I took a leave of absence from my teaching at The American University to work as an Associate Director to the Assistant to the President at the White House during the Carter Administration. My primary responsibilities were in the area of speechwriting and assisting in the development and articulation of the President's National Urban Policy Initiative. It was at the White House where I first heard the story (which I have encounted many times since) of why, immediately after his inauguration, President John F. Kennedy requested signed, but undated, letters of resignation from all of his principal administration officials and White House staff members. When asked to explain why he undertook such an unorthodox course of action, he simply and straightforwardly answered: "I never want to *ask* for a letter of resignation from a subordinate, I only want to *accept* it." I seriously doubt that such a policy engendered a high degree of sincerity or security among the President's key advisors.

By contrast, justices of the Supreme Court and members of both houses of Congress are indeed peers, bound together by traditions of collegiality and the need to promote an atmosphere of competitive understanding and support. What mostly separates them from each other in terms of power and influence is their seniority and their respective committee assignments. Peerage provides members of the Court and Congress with the freedom to argue passionately and disagree among themselves privately and publicly (generally with the intent toward achieving communal resolution regarding the issue at hand) without the risk of losing either their power or their position.

Often, for members of the White House staff, the cabinet, and the rest of his administration, the president is mistakenly perceived by them as "king" and thus as his loyal subordinates they find themselves dutifully serving him as "courtiers" with an understandable (though hardly helpful) proclivity toward expression of servile sycophancy. Additionally, the president and his advisors frequently begin to see Congress as 535 independent "barons" who must be reminded to submit to the authority of the nation's rightful ruler. Such an adversarial situation usually degenerates into being an arena of combative divisiveness which rapidly becomes a detriment to the president and to the citizens that he was elected to serve.

In Albert Speer's highly acclaimed 1970 autobiography, *Inside The Third Reich*, he mentions:

> "There is a special trap for every holder of power, whether the director of a company, the head of a state, or the ruler of a dictatorship. His favor is so desirable to his subordinates that they will sue for it by every means possible. Servility becomes endemic among his entourage, who compete among themselves in their show of devotion. This in turn exercises a sway upon the ruler, who becomes corrupted in his turn."

He continues:

> "The key to the quality of the man in power is how he reacts to this situation. I have observed a number of industrialists and military men who knew how to fend off this danger. Where power has been exercised over generations, a kind of hereditary incorruptibility grows up. Only a few individuals among those around Hitler withstood the temptation to sycophancy. Hitler himself put up no visible resistance to the evolution of a court."

Many have come to criticize members of the Clinton Administration because of their alleged arrogance, relative youth, and inexperience in understanding the peculiar ways of transacting power and advancing policy initiatives in the nation's capital. This is really not the problem. Older and wiser individuals, willing to be more deferential to the expectations and eccentricities of the Washington establishment power elite, are always readily (and enthusiastically) available to replace any or all of those presently in office. However, what cannot be so easily overcome are the problems that are indigenous to the presidency itself.

Generally speaking, some of our most successful presidents (Washington, Jefferson, Madison, Lincoln, and Franklin Roosevelt, to name a few) were leaders who were supremely confident in their capacity to confront and overcome the challenges placed before them and who wisely surrounded themselves with intelligent, loyal, strong-willed

competent individuals who were awarded the opportunity to respect-
fully speak their minds on the most sensitive of subjects without fear of
reprisal or threat of removal. Only in such a collegial community of
common commitment can presidents receive the substantive support
and service that they rightfully deserve.

What every president needs closest to him is a wise, talented, and
tenacious individual who can serve as a kind of presidential "provost"
whose role is to foster forthright communication within the administration (at its highest and lowest levels) so that it can better understand its
mission and the need to improve and expand its methods of meshing its
message with the hearts and minds and expectations of average
citizens.

The International Debt Problem: The Case of Argentina Revisited

by Michael Adamson

At the end of 1990, after a half century of mismanagement, the seventh richest nation on earth in 1930 was 70th. In the decade of 1990, inflation averaged 450 percent. At its peak, in early 1990, it exceeded 20,000 percent on an annual basis. Gross domestic product (GDP) per head fell by more than 20 percent and was down by half since 1930. Manufacturing as a percentage of GDP had fallen to levels last seen in the 1940s ("History in," 1992). Investment fell to eight percent of GDP, down from 23 percent in 1980 ("Nearly time," 1992). Yet, two years later, the Argentine economy was hardly recognizable.

The stockmarket in Buenos Aires posted the largest gain in dollar terms of any bourse in the world in 1991 (more than 400 percent). Monetary stability had cut inflation down to size. Bankrupt public sector firms were being auctioned off. The increasingly open economy was on its way to a second consecutive year of five percent plus growth. The government was shrinking and the budget was in surplus.

Where the Radical Party under Raul Alfonsin spent seven years wandering in the desert of economic disaster, the Peronist government under Carlos Menem engineered a remarkable, if not improbable, restoration of the economy by reducing the role of the state, freeing trade and relying on individual action as the engine of economic growth. The events comprising this return to market-based policies are reviewed here in the context of the international debt saga of the 1980s. It illustrates what is necessary for the revival of developing nations in Eastern Europe, the former Soviet Union and elsewhere in the world. It is also relevant to the fate of the world's richest economies, including the United States, as they struggle with the problems created by interventionist governments.

71

Lincoln Review

INTO THE ABYSS, 1983–1989

From 1973–84, government expenditures under Peronist and military rule grew from 16.7 percent of GDP to 35.2 (International Financial Statistics, 1981, 1984). The budget deficit for this period averaged 5.2 percent of GDP. The ultimate effect of these policies was a worsening balance of payments problem as deficit spending was largely financed by taking on ever more external debt.

The military government which took power in 1976 assumed an external debt of $8.3 billion. In their seven years of rule, an additional $20 billion was borrowed in the public sector, leaving the Alfonsin government in December, 1983 with the world's highest inflation rate, a budget deficit exceeding 13 percent of GNP and the third largest external debt among developing nations.

Argentina had little to show for its $43.6 billion debt in terms of productive investment. Its highly protected and regulated economy, coupled with the absence of internal markets, allowed the military government to waste borrowed funds on prestige and ill-considered projects with little or not economic value.

The government was left with an unproductive economy and unmanageable levels of debt service obligations. The road to economic revival and the ability to repay foreign creditors lay in releasing the chains on the economy, including the reduction of public sector expenditure and the restriction of the government's role in the economy. It was a road not taken.

Mr. Alfonsin promised that the government would fight the triple digit inflation rate and sell or close hundreds of state-owned companies, reduce public sector spending and encourage private investment (Ulman, 1984). Yet, his Radical Party never applied its own proposals to restore economic health. The government was politically unwilling to take on Peronist trade unions. It spent precious political capital attempting to bring rebellious soldiers smarting from the 1982 Falklands War to trial for alleged human rights abuses of the 1970s. No measures were introduced which improved the economy, reduced the 60 percent share of industrial activity directly controlled by the public sector, freed trade, lowered inflation or reduced the external debt exposure. Indeed, the state of the economy was even more precarious at the end of Radical Party rule in 1989 than it was in 1983. The 1980s were truly a lost decade.

The headlines from the Alfonsin years read like a never ending nightmare. Plan Austral was introduced in July, 1985. It employed wage and price controls coupled with the introduction of a new currency pegged to the dollar, the austral. In April, 1986, direct controls were relaxed in the face of union pressures, whose members' real wages were falling steadily. The austral was devalued several times to prevent it from becoming ludicrously overvalued against the dollar. By August, 1986 inflation was up to 150 percent per year ("Taming the," 1986).

Inflation reached 322 percent in July, 1987. "An unhappy mixture of British-style trade unions and Italian-style public finances" resulted in a lost battle against inflation ("Hype on," 1988, p. 63). Public enterprises continued to spill red ink. Provincial government spending was out of control. The budget deficit for 1987 was seven percent of GDP. The austral fell precipitously against the dollar. Increasingly impoverished union members resorted to widespread strikes. While total debt outstanding fell to $49.4 billion from $50.8 billion in 1985, interest as a percent of exports had increased to 33.1 from 25.4 percent ("Muddling through," 1988).

Meanwhile, debt service obligations grew. In 1988, they totaled $4.7 billion on $56 billion total debt. The government, rather than going to the heart of the problem, i.e., the economic distortions it was perpetuating, sought new money from the World Bank and the International Monetary Fund (IMF). It promised to cut the budget deficit to 2.9 percent and drop most agricultural export taxes ("Another year," 1988).

Instead, the budget deficit soared, driven to 10 percent of GDP by bloated, loss-making public firms. The IMF cancelled $450 million of a standby loan for not meeting agreed-to macroeconomic targets. Inflation threatened to become hyperinflation. Privatization programs floated by the government were resisted by Peronist trade unions. The government was unwilling to negotiate debt for equity swaps as had been done successfully in Chile ("Awaiting the," 1988).

At the end of 1988, the austral was worth five percent of its original value. By April, 1989, monthly inflation rates were running between 50–60 percent. Argentina was at least $2.5 billion in arrears on interest payments to commercial banks ("Don't cry," 1989).

The government had rescheduled its debt for a third time since 1982 in September, 1988, taking on $1.25 billion in new loans from the World Bank. Yet, both the IMF and World Bank now suspended credit lines. The failure of the Alfonsin government to establish free markets and not debauch the currency was complete. Total debt stocks stood at more than $64 billion (World Bank, 1991). Radical Party rule left a legacy of protectionism, subsidized state ownership of enterprise, misallocated resources, huge budget deficits and spiraling inflation. Program after program put forth to combat inflation had merely attacked its symptoms through wage and price controls, invariably renounced, rather than its causes. In the run-up to the May elections, "hyperinflation and the scramble for physical goods were well under way ("Don't cry," 1989, p. 71)."

THE ROAD FROM SERFDOM, 1989–1992

When Carlos Menem assumed power, 17 percent of the work force was employed by state-owned firms. The political economy was characterized by an insolvent social security system, profligate provincial governments, an incompetent civil service and a woeful education system. Prominent among loss-making public companies, the national railway was managing to lose twice as much as it earned in revenues ("History in," 1992). A half century of bad government had run Argentina down "from affluence to shabbiness ("Power cut", 1989, p. 39)."

As a Peronist preaching a populist message in the campaign, Mr. Menem was not expected to lead the country to free market reform. Indeed, actions early in his administration pointed to more of the same policies which had brought the economy to its knees.

Though he promised to fight inflation and to privatize state firms (over the complaints from Peronist trade unions), attempts at privatization and cutting the public sector payroll were "haphazard and clumsy ("Marital blitz," 1990, p. 38)." The continuing lack of restraint over the money supply was painfully familiar. Inflation was 3,103 percent in 1989 and 2,314 percent in 1990 (Baker, 1992).

By the end of 1990, though, policies to control inflation and restore economic freedom were under way. Privatization of the telephone utility and the state airline raised $7 billion toward paying off the external debt. After Domingo Cavallo was made finance minister in January, 1991, reforms accelerated. As a Peronist himself, Mr. Menem was able to use his political power to keep the unions at bay. The austral was made fully convertible in April, 1991 and the monetary base was backed 100 percent by gold and foreign currency reserves. Indexation of wages and other contracts was prohibited.

On October 31, 1991, measures were announced which

> banned all restrictions on sales of goods and services, deregulated road freight, closed down the national grain and meat boards and a flock other state agencies, did away with most regulations and taxes on imports and exports, told the ports to stay open 24 hours a day, ordered customs officials not to block trade and . . . lifted restrictions on the imports and retail sales of medicine ("The starting," 1991).

Argentina now was one of the most open economies in the world, according to the GATT. Inflation was down to 1.5 percent per month. The economy grew at five percent in 1991. The budget deficit was cut to 1.8 percent of GDP in 1991, from five percent in 1990 and an average of nine percent during the 1980s ("Nearly time," 1992).

By April, 1992, in addition to the telephone utility and the state airline, two television stations, 10,000 kilometers of roads and some railway lines had been privatized. Everything was now on the auction block, including the electricity, gas, and water systems and the balance of the rail system. Even the oil industry was opened up to foreign firms, though state ownership of YPF, the state oil company, is to be retained through 1993. Privatization not only cut external debt totals (in the form of debt for equity swaps), it permanently reduced the burden of annual public sector corporate losses, which used to account for half the total budget deficit.

The revival is not complete. It remains for long-cosseted industries to get back to the business of producing goods and services which are competitive on world markets. Inflation, though falling, remains above U.S. levels. The government is holding firm against a devaluation of the currency, putting the onus on companies to cut costs. Clearly, though, balanced budgets, free trade, privatization and monetary control have set the stage for the revival of the economy. On the strength of its economy, Argentina was able to successfully renegotiate $31 billion in debt obligations in the space of two months in early 1992 (Hirshberger, 1992).

LESSONS FROM THE DEBT DEBACLE

When Mexico announced in August, 1982 its inability to service interest obligations on its external debt, international attention focused on the financial problems this posed to the banking system, the collapse of which was thought by many to be imminent. The commercial banks and their governments sought to avert this primarily through the IMF. The IMF served as the conduit through which debt repayments were rescheduled. This generally entailed agreeing to an austerity plan. The interest payments of over 30 nations were thus renegotiated in return for promises to reduce budget deficits and pursue export-oriented growth policies. The collapse of the banking system indeed never happened. Focusing the attention on the international finance aspect of the problem, though, served to stay the day of reckoning when interventionist governments had to do something about the disastrous policies they were pursuing.

Certainly, from the strictly financial point of view, several factors external to the debtor nations precipitated the 1982 crisis. The dollar rebounded on currency exchanges in the early 1980s as the United

States adopted monetary policies designed to fight inflation and turned heretofore negative real interest rates positive. The 1979 hike in oil prices strained the balance of payments of nations which borrowed liberally in the 1970s. Increasingly protectionist trade measures, particularly in agriculture, exacerbated the problem by closing potential avenues of trade with American and European economies. All served to overwhelm the capability of many nations to service existing external debt levels.

By 1988, however, multinational agencies, including the World Bank and the IMF, were making only $6 billion in new loans and were collecting $26 billion in interest payments ("The banks'," 1989). Capital flows had reversed from the 1970s, when so-called petrodollars from the nations of OPEC, enriched from the 1973 oil embargo, flowed to developing nations. Market debt reduction schemes were allowing banks to reduce their exposure. The focus of the problem shifted to the political stability and economic policies of the debtor nations, the real problem all along.

The international debt problems of the 1980s were symptoms of the greater disease, namely government control of economic activity. The levels of debt which were sinking the economies of Latin America and Africa were proportionally no greater than those of Canada and Australia, or of the United States 80 years earlier. They were less as a percentage of GDP than those successfully being serviced by the strong market economies of South Korea and Taiwan. The wounds incurred by the Argentinas of the world were largely self-inflicted (Forbes, 1989).

The solution"instead of a thousand-and-one-debt plans is for governments to get their policies right, which means having fewer of them (Crook, 1989, p. 56)." That the governments of debtor nations hadn't been getting their policies in order was shown by the stampede of funds which poured into bank accounts of the countries from which they originated. For Argentina, this amounted to some $46 billion, roughly three fourths of the external debt outstanding.

Only economic reforms bring this money back, because monetary stability overcomes capital flow problems associated with high inflation, i.e., individuals refuse to hold assets in the local currency, buying dollars and shipping them abroad instead. Individuals don't have to be taught that profligate governments steal their savings and deprive them of their property rights ("History in," 1992).

Politicians often state that government intervention in an economy is necessary to address imperfect markets. They assume that government is competent and able to improve on markets. What the economic histories of developing nations show is that markets, whatever their imperfections, function better than inept governments. Unfortunately, the list of nations that have suffered decades of misery at the hands of incompetent governments is extensive. No amount of development aid, loans, or debt restructuring can overcome this (Crook, 1989).

The debt experiences of the 1980s also bring into question the merits of IMF and World Bank involvement. Neither institution has the resources to alter the direction of any nation's economy (Crook, 1989). At best, they serve to smooth out short term balance of payments problems and soothe the nerves of commercial banks and their governments. Since this often involves an assumption of risk on the part of the taxpayers of the creditor nations, their role can hardly be applauded. In addition, their funds are not directly invested in entrepreneurial ventures seeking to implement new ideas, but funnelled through the very same governments who caused the problems in the first place (Forbes, 1989). As the market institutions to address debt reduction become more sophisticated, the rationale behind their institutional fixes becomes even less defensible.

Nor are global schemes such as the Baker and Brady plans likely to produce lasting reform. The Baker Plan, announced in 1985 by James Baker, the U.S. Treasury Secretary, encouraged new private and public lending to refinance interest payments while emphasizing growth-oriented adjustments in debtor nation policies. The Brady Plan (proposed by Nicholas Brady, U.S. Treasury Secretary under George Bush), a debt reduction plan floated in 1989, ended the assumption held by lending institutions that debtor nations would eventually service their debts in full (Nowzad, 1990). Commercial banks forgave a portion of their loans in return for other concessions, namely that the balance of the debt would be serviced. Both reinforced the resources of the IMF with World Bank and other multilateral institution funds. Both were the ultimate strategies in buying time. Ironically, these plans were quite similar to several such schemes put forth during the debt crisis of the 1930s, none of which succeeded: In the 1930s, as in the 1980s, countries which made economic and fiscal reforms were better able to repay their debt obligations (Eichengreen, 1991).

In a previous article, I concluded that the only way out for Argentina from her external debt quagmire was a return to a free market economy, where the role of government is limited to setting the rules that protect property rights and where the decisions of individuals drive an expanding and ever more productive economy (Adamson, 1985). At the time, there appeared little hope that such reforms would ever be enacted. The political economy of Argentina in 1985 was an apt demonstration of the extent to which government manipulation of economic activity leads to ever lower standards of living and the rending of the social fabric.

The more recent events reviewed here show how quickly the removal

77

Lincoln Review

of market distortions results in the return to a productive economy and the ability to repay debts. Argentina is at the brink of an astounding revival. It is an experience the citizens of the United States, the world's largest debtor nation, would do well to learn from as they grapple with various schemes peddled by their government to address chronic budget deficits in the 1990s. The debt debacle of the 1980s was not unique. Whenever and wherever governments shackle markets and individuals, it will be repeated.

REFERENCES

Adamson, Michael. "The International Debt Problem: The Case of Argentina." *The Freeman* (December, 1985): 732–736.

"Another year older." *The Economist,* March 26, 1988, pp. 78, 82.

"Awaiting the receivers." *The Economist,* August 6, 1988, pp. 57–58.

Baker, Stephen; Charters, Ann; Smith, Geri; and Weiner, Elizabeth. "The Big Move to Free Markets." *Business Week,* June 15, 1992, pp. 50–55.

Crook, Clive. "Poor man's burden." *The Economist,* survey, September 23, 1989.

"Don't cry for me, Weimar." *The Economist,* April 29, 1989, pp. 71–72.

Eichengreen, Barry. "Historical Research on International Lending and Debt." *Journal of Economic Perspectives* 5 (Spring, 1991): 149–169.

Forbes, Malcolm S., Jr. "Self-Made Crisis." *Forbes,* February 20, 1989, p. 27.

Hirshberger, Bill. "Argentina's master of reform." *Institutional Investor* 26 (May, 1992): 87–92.

"History in the Making?" *Euromoney,* supplement, February, 1992, pp. 1–8.

International Monetary Fund. *International Financial Statistics: 1981, 1984.* Washington, D.C., 1981, 1984.

"Marital blitz." *The Economist,* June 23, 1990, p. 38.

"Muddling through." *The Economist,* February 6, 1988, p. 80.

"Nearly time to tango." *The Economist,* April 18, 1992, pp. 17–20.

Nowzad, Bahram. "Lessons of the Debt Decade." *Finance and Development* (March, 1990): 9–13.

"Power cut." *The Economist,* January 14, 1989, pp. 39–40.

"Taming the beast." *The Economist,* November 15, 1986, pp. 55–64.

"The banks' great escape." *The Economist,* February 11, 1989, pp. 73–74.

"The starting gun." *The Economist,* November 9, 1991.

Ulman, Neil. "Argentina Lists Plans to Curb Deficit, Inflation." *Wall Street Journal,* January 27, 1984, p. 35.

World Bank. *World Debt Tables, 1991.* Washington, D.C., 1991.

Black America's
Conservative Public Policy Journal

LINCOLN REVIEW
The Journal of The Lincoln Institute
for Research and Education
"America's Leading Conservative Black Think-Tank"

J.A. Parker
Editor

Seychelles · Private Property · Welfare · Third World · Education Vouchers · Ghana · South Africa · United Nations · Bussing · Namibia · Reaganomics · Inflation · Flat Tax · Soviet Union · Right To Work · Labor Policy · Davis-Bacon · Right to Life · Quotas · Angola · Kenya · Hunger · Minimum Wage · Zimbabwe · Cuba · Crime · East-West Trade · Homeless · Ronald Reagan · Tax Indexing · Martin Luther King · Deregulation · Social Security · Voting Rights · Affirmative Action · National Defense

Essays of Note

The Market's Easy Touch

by Joseph S. Fulda

A few years back, yet another phenomenon emerged to lacerate the sensibilities of the common folk stuck in the inner cities: Radios blaring at all hours of the day and night. In addition to the obvious assault on the quality of life in the poorer neighborhoods, the maximum-volume radios aggravated racial tensions for the simple reason that most of the radio-owners were minority youths in their teens and twenties. In my own neighborhood—Spanish Harlem in New York City—derogatory comments about the traditionally out-of-doors Hispanic culture abounded.

People of all persuasions, especially older folk, began to fight back. Soon the city-run subway and surface transit systems sported large red-on-white signs, "No Radio Playing." Then, police were authorized to seize radios while they were blaring (as evidence, not civil forfeiture). Decent folks took on an us-or-them attitude towards the minority youths that were typically at the center of the problem, and race-relations took a giant step backwards.

Along came SONY, and with its well-known ingenuity and inventiveness, a new product was placed on the market: the Walkman. Soon, blaring radios became a thing of the past as people of all ages and ethnic backgrounds enjoyed music on trains, buses, and streets alike, while walking, riding, or simply sitting on park benches. Users of this product clearly enjoyed having their immediate surroundings suffused with music, possible before the Walkman only with the offensive maximum-volume radios. SONY did what it does best: It identified a real need—environment-suffusing music which doesn't disturb the neighbors—and filled it with a new product.

81

Lincoln Review

Today, blaring radios are a rarity; youths and older folks, minorities and whites, all use Walkmans or the many imitations that the market has spawned. And, the racially tinged angry comments of yesteryear have been proven wrong. SONY's success shows the difference between the easy touch of the market response to social problems and the heavy-handed state response to quality-of-life issues. SONY has been rewarded with profits for its genteel product. And, "Walkman" is now an entry in the 1993 (10th) edition of the Merriam-Webster dictionary—just see page 1329!

An Open Letter to My Children

Tibor R. Machan

Dearest Kids:

There are so many things that you need to prepare for in order to have just a reasonably contented life that I feel sad that about the following topic I need to talk with you in a special way.

As you know, I was born and raised in Hungary. Other members of your family, too, are descendants of recent emigrants from Europe. Your parents were not alive and few of their parents were living in this country when slavery and segregation were legal and practiced by many people who were white, as well as approved of by some who did not themselves hold slaves or practice segregation.

Nevertheless, in our day—and I am writing this in late 1992—some people believe that you and I are all responsible, in some measure, for slavery and segregation, neither of which did you have anything to do with. Nor did your parents! None of us, in short, was guilty of perpetrating or supporting the evils of slavery and segregation. But these people do not care about this. They look at you and see that you are what they loosely call white or Caucasian and declare that you are guilty of racism.

Recently, a listener wrote to the National Public Radio network about how he himself, who is white, is a racist—and NPR allowed him to read his letter for the entire country to hear. The listener used the phrase, "I am getting over my racism," as if racism were a disease from which he is recovering.

Even to honor such a remark with being selected for broadcasting is evidence of gross confusion. To begin with, simply being white can never make anyone a racist. Some sadly vicious or gutless persons say such bizarre things, holding all whites collectively responsible for whatever ails non-whites, be it a result of racism or of anything else. But it cannot be true. Why?

First, because if being white made one a racist, there would be nothing morally wrong with racism, any more than there is anything morally wrong with having curly hair because one is black or being sensitive to solar exposure because one is white. Whatever one cannot help being is something no one can be—and should ever permit oneself to feel—guilty for. This extends to being born to white or black parents, to parents who are well off or being endowed with natural good looks or lacking in it. Being what one is by birth is just not something that is or could ever be one's fault.

Whatever some people loudly proclaim, millions of whites in the United States of America had not only no hand in slavery or segregation laws but hadn't even had any relatives who did. The view that being white makes one guilty and deserves the imposition of various kinds of burdens is utterly false, not to mention a form of injustice exactly identical to what racism toward anyone amounts to. It is morally confused to hold someone guilty for being black or yellow or anything one cannot help being and it is morally evil to make that confusion respectable. I hope that when you think this through it will be clear to you.

Please consider very seriously never to accept any opinion that identifies you as a racist only because you are white. If, of course, you have prejudices, irrational opinions either favorable or unfavorable to blacks or members of any other color or ethnic group, then you are racist and you deserve scorn and should feel guilt. But not for any other reason.

Furthermore, never be afraid to disagree with members of any other racial group different from the one you happen to belong to—even about issues involving them. You can fully evaluate their arguments, regardless of your or their skin color, their ethnic or national origin. Race, color or such origins makes no one right or wrong—to think otherwise is indeed racist. To fail to air your disagreements to such persons would often be a sign of disrespect. They should be as ready to handle your views as you are ready to handle theirs.

Here is another thing: It is hard to think of any person whose ancestors had not been victimized by some people. These, in turn, produced offspring who may well have benefited a bit from that oppression. To complain about that forever is pointless and perhaps even devious. It will, if continued and widespread, return us to prehistoric tribal barbarism—and the clannishness of the Mafia—in which the children of the children of the aggrieved had to mete out punishment to the children of the children of the transgressors. It was one of the noble achievements of the American Founding Fathers to have laid down principles of political justice in the Declaration of Independence that could guide us toward the ultimate rejection of such group-think human relations. Now, mostly at the hands of those who have revived group-think and collective guilt, America is being nudged away from the Founders' conception of a decent human society toward the state of war of all groups against all other groups.

If one is not a racist—if one does not judge others by biological or genetic traits or characteristics over which they have no control—and judges others by the content of their character (to recall Martin Luther King's very precise phrase), one should not sit still for the nonsensical racist lambaste unleashed these days by half-educated people. One should also realize that what lies behind current racial strife is the ill conceived effort to remedy past ills by way of group-think: affirmative action, proportionate allocation of positions that require, instead, attention to competence, hiring and admission quotas, etc. These ill conceived policies have resulted in pitting groups united on trivial matters against other similar groups. It has also slowed down considerably the development of a racially and ethnically neutral culture wherein what counts is how well one performs, not what (race, ethnic group, or national origin) one happens to be.

Of course, you will have your own ideas to offer about all this. But I, as your father, believe it is my responsibility to indicate to you clearly what I think about this matter, as I do about some others. That is partly what parents have to do—to educate their children about values. And justice is certainly a value that is now being threatened in ways different from how it was threatened and violated in the past.

Your loving father.

ODE TO A DEAD TREE

Gary North

I think that I shall never see
A sight as lovely as a tree:
A tree cut down for pulp and boards,
Cut down for profit and rewards.

Whenever forests disappear
To fill a bookstore front to rear,
The angels sing a glorious song,
Especially if the books are long.

When trees grow high above the earth
I love to estimate their worth.
I praise the chainsaw and the axe,
Converting trees to paperbacks.

I love to contemplate bare hills,
Solutions to society's ills.
For every tree dragged out by hooks
May soon become a shelf of books.

When men cry "Timber!" I rejoice,
A perfect use for human voice.
The sound of buzz saws is symphonic
So long as books remain dendronic.

I think of trees throughout the ages
Especially as I'm turning pages:
Majestic trees in ageless mists
Transformed into best-sellers' lists.

Down my spine I get the shivers:
Giant forests into slivers!
Forests growing through long winters;
Spring will see them all in splinters.

The thought of trees cut down for wood,
Serving man as nature should,
Literate mankind now confesses:
"Cut the trees and start the presses!"

Lincoln Reviews

**Forbidden Grounds: The Case
Against Employment
Discrimination Laws**
by Richard A. Epstein
Harvard University Press
530 pages
$39.95

When the Civil Rights Act of 1964 was being debated in Congress, Sen. Barry Goldwater opposed it and said that he did not have "a racist bone" in his body. He may be vindicated soon.

Forbidden Grounds: The Case Against Employment Discrimination Laws by Richard A. Epstein, James Parker Hall Distinguished Service Professor of Law at the University of Chicago, is a dispassionate, comprehensive, and bold critique of the laws (the Equal Pay Act of 1963, the Civil Rights Act of 1964, the Age Discrimination in Employment Act of 1967, and the Americans with Disabilities Act of 1990) conceived to remedy past discrimination because of race, sex, age, and disability and to prohibit new occurrences. Being astute in the law, philosophy, and economics, he systematically launches a frontal assault on the ideological, legal, and moral justifications of the laws inspired to root out those practices. Noticeably absent, and undoubtedly to the dismay of many readers, are the treatments of discrimination due to sexual orientation and ac-

cess to public accommodations (although mentioned, not the subject of this book); but seeing how Epstein persistently applies libertarian private property rights theory to the cutting issues of our time, as he did in *Takings: Private Property and the Power of Eminent Domain*, could sexual orientation and public accommodations be far behind?

Drawing from the philosophers Hobbes, Hume, Locke, and Blackstone, Epstein begins Part I by documenting the philosophical foundations of man's nature, social theory, and common law. Controlling coercion, the determination of ownership, freedom of contract, and the antidiscrimination laws form the basis of his argument. Epstein should be commended for making these his starting points, as well they should be in any honest treatment of any laws regulating discrimination and the use of private property in a free society. He defines victims of force and discrimination, explains the natural limits on discrimination, and presents rational discrimination in competitive markets as an integral component of decision-making processes and cost-benefit analyses. The author treats discrimination objectively, since it does not exclusively refer to invidious or tendentious perceptions and reactions to immutable human characteristics such as race or sex, but it refers to judicious, discerning, or differentiating thinking or behavior. He concludes Part I by discussing monopoly via the restriction of entry into markets and employment situations.

In Part II, Epstein outlines a brief history of the police power with respect to race between 1890 and 1937, the period of federal regulatory revolution in 1937 to the Civil Rights Act of 1964, and the constitutional challenges to the Civil Rights Act of 1964. He explodes certain misconceptions about how labor and employment markets functioned during Reconstruction and Jim Crow. For example, southern state governments forced companies and individuals to behave in ways which ran counter to their own best interests, and in ways in which they would not have otherwise acted if free economic and political environments had existed by restricting free entry and free employment relationships. Certain states mandated inefficiencies to the detriment of employees and customers alike. This is not to say that racial and sexual bigotry did not exist, but that the control of key governmental institutions like the courts, licensing boards, and agencies artificially increased the abusive power of the state and simultaneously marginalized the efficient operations of the markets.

Epstein then takes on race discrimination in Part III. From slavery through Jim Crow, through the civil rights struggles of the sixties, to the current tensions over affirmative action, race has played a vital role in the formulation of civil rights law and in government sponsored retributive action inspired to redress past grievances. Epstein deals with contracts at will, notes their preferred status and functional advantages in the marketplace, and he provides detailed reviews of landmark Supreme Court decisions regarding race, disparate treatment, and disparate impact.

He gives a legislative history of Title VII of the 1964 Civil Rights Act and shows how the high court inconsistently construed the antidiscrimination provisions of the Act, depending on the contexts. In addition to explaining how the Act interfered with markets, Epstein reveals that some judicial constructions contradicted the antidiscrimination norm prescribed by the Act's authors. The legislators specifically proscribed preferential treatment because they foresaw that it would be unfair and that it would have deleterious effects if enacted. Unfortunately, all three branches of government have since acquiesced to using preferential treatment as a means of attempting to enforce equal opportunity. One positive outcome of the Civil Rights Act of 1964, Epstein acknowledges, was the abolition of government sponsored discrimination, thereby allowing blacks and other groups to gain access to institutions previously denied them.

Part IV is a critique of sex discrimination including an excellent illustration of why race and sex discrimination are misleading parallels. Both markets and the sexes fair much better when people are free to recognize and consider the biological, social, and cultural differences between men and women when making business and employment decisions. Many business owners are well aware of the legitimate cost differentials between the sexes when they are inextricably linked to bona fide occupational qualifications, which, unfortunately, most government policy makers and bureaucrats are oblivious to and are ill-suited to respect because of their being distant from everyday business transactions and the complexities of the work place.

Epstein treats pensions, pregnancy, and sexual harassment objectively, free of the stridency and emotionalism which so frequently characterize current discussions of these issues. He strongly urges the government to take a hands-off approach to economic transactions involving sex differences, and he recommends that the courts and legislators apply contract and common law to sexual harassment and not to adjudicate it any differently than molestation or assault.

Part V is a stunning argument against affirmative action because it is a contravention to the antidiscrimination norm advanced by the 1964 Civil Rights Act it purports to reaffirm. While Epstein believes there is no place for affirmative action in public institutions, he believes it should be allowed in the private sector if employers choose to use it as in the Steelworkers v. Weber case. His recommendation to those who desire to effectuate affirmative action is novel and is sure to surprise many people.

In Part VI, Epstein cites the Age Discrimination in Employment Act of 1967 and the Americans with Disabilities Act (ADA) of 1990 as injecting additional regulations which do more harm than good by adding more costs to doing business which everyone, i.e. employers, customers, and intended beneficiaries, must bear. He examines the use of mandatory retirement in business and in higher education and defends them from government prohibition. He challenges tenure at colleges and universities because many professors who would otherwise retire or move on to positions at other institutions crowd out younger up-and-coming teaching talent and they also create undo burdens on pension programs. According to Epstein, the ADA imposes excessive costs on business by requiring them to accommodate the disabled, whether or not businesses will ever encounter them as employees or customers, e.g. by requiring them to remove architectural barriers such as narrow door openings and to provide ramps for wheelchairs. Many architects welcome that change in the law. This law has

Lincoln Review

also created an economic burden on employers who would be required to carry insurance for employees having the HIV (or any other preexisting medical condition).

Epstein writes "it is thus simply ruinous to require any employers, as the ADA stipulates, to issue life and health insurance to HIV-positive workers (or even workers likely to become HIV-positive) on the same terms and conditions under which it issues insurance coverage to the rest of its work force. The magnitude of the risk is such that the premiums required to cover HIV-positive workers may well exceed the salaries they earn."

In the tradition of Hayek and Sowell, Richard Epstein delivers a cogent and riveting indictment of government sponsored central planning and bureaucratic egalitarianism in the guise of the employment antidiscrimination laws. Although he does not explicitly call for the complete abolition of the Equal Employment Opportunity Commission, which many libertarians would probably welcome, Epstein does advocate the repeal of all employment antidiscrimination laws.

The prescriptions in *Forbidden Grounds* are bound to unnerve many a liberal and, for that matter, a few conservatives, by challenging their benevolent sensibilities of equality, fairness, and justice. Where freedom of contract and private property rights form the legal infrastructure of our constitutional regime, the complete enforcement of the antidiscrimination norm would portend ominous things.

Epstein captures this idea in his conclusion: "the totalitarian implications become clear only when one realizes the excessive steps that must be taken to enforce the antidiscrimination principle in favor of some groups while it is overtly ignored relative to other groups. It is not the least of the ironies of the study of Title VII [of the 1964 Civil Rights Act] that has brought in its wake more discrimination (and for less good purpose) than would exist in an unregulated system."

While *Forbidden Grounds* may destroy any remaining, albeit small, possibility of a Supreme Court nomination for Epstein, this piercing critique is must reading for all businessmen, policy makers, and anyone interested in civil rights, private property rights, and, yes, equality under the law.

We may now understand what Barry foresaw and reasoned all along.

—*Carlton L. Eugene*

The Politics of Prudence
by Russell Kirk
Intercollegiate Studies Institute
(14 South Bryn Mawr Avenue,
Bryn Mawr, Pa. 19010),
304 Pages,
$19.95.

In the history of civilization, a period of decay is followed by a period of renewal.

Ours, surely, is a period of decay. All around us are the signs of disintegration. Crime is rampant, drug abuse is widespread, abortions in many communities exceed live births. American families are in a state of disarray with half of marriages ending in divorce and, in the minority community, the vast majority of children born out of wedlock. Our schools are failing to teach, our criminal justice system is failing to punish the guilty, and disillusionment with our public and political life is widespread.

If ever there was a need for a conservative response to such a descent into decadence, this appears to be such a time. In this noteworthy new book, Russell Kirk, one of America's leading thinkers whose book *The Conservative Mind* is thought by many to have sparked the modern conservative movement, expresses the hope that the 21st century may see the kind of renewal we so desperately need.

Part of the problem of the modern world, Kirk believes, has been its commitment to "ideology," whether it be communist, Nazi, fascist, socialist, welfare state or some other variety. He commends, instead, political prudence, one of the four "classical virtues," as opposed to "ideology," a word that signifies political fanaticism.

In the initial chapters, some of which were delivered as lectures at the Heritage Foundation in Washington, D.C., he outlines the principles of conservative thought, summarizes important conservative books and offers brief accounts of eminent conservatives, among them Cicero, Marcus Aurelius, Samuel Johnson, Sir Walter Scott, T.S. Eliot and Nathaniel Hawthorne. He analyzes conservative factions in contemporary America and contemplates the manner in which a decadent society may be saved from its own worst impulses.

This volume, he tells us, is meant to be a "defense of prudential politics as opposed to ideological politics. The author hopes to persuade the rising generation to set their faces against political fanaticism and utopian schemes, by which the world has been afflicted since 1914. 'Politics is the art of the possible,' the conservative says; he thinks of political policies as intended to preserve order, justice and freedom. The ideologue, on the contrary, thinks of politics as a revolutionary instrument for transforming society and even transforming human nature. In the march toward Utopia, the ideologue is merciless."

The ideologies which have been so costly in our time—communism, fascism and Nazism—are, Kirk points out, really "inverted religions." But, he notes, "the prudential politician knows that 'Utopia' means 'Nowhere'; that we cannot march to an earthly Zion; that human nature and hu-

91

man institutions are imperfectible; that aggressive 'righteousness' in politics ends in slaughter. True religion is a discipline for the soul, not for the state . . . It is the conservative leader who, setting his face against all ideologies, is guided by what Patrick Henry called 'the lamp of experience.' In this 20th century, it has been the body of opinion generally called 'conservative' that has defended the Permanent Things from ideological assaults."

Conservatism, Kirk writes, "is not a bundle of theories got up by some closet philosopher. On the contrary, the conservative conviction grows out of experience: the experience of the species, of the nation, of the person . . . It is the practical statesman, rather than the visionary recluse, who has maintained a healthy tension between the claims of authority and the claims of freedom. . . . The Constitution of the United States, two centuries old, is a sufficient example of the origin of conservative constitutions in a people's experience . . . the Constitution . . . was rooted in direct personal experience of the political and social institutions which had developed in the Thirteen Colonies since the middle of the 17th century, and in thorough knowledge of the British growth, over seven centuries, of parliamentary government, ordered freedom and the rule of law."

Now, as the 20th century wanes, the evidence of decline is all around us, a situation not dis-similar to Greece and Rome in their last days. The very idea of "culture," argues Kirk, comes from the "cult," and, "For the past three centuries, the cult of our civilization, that is the Christian religion, has been declining in power . . . the elaborate culture we have known stands in grave peril."

The triumph of ideology would, Kirk notes, be the triumph of what Edmund Burke called the "antagonist world." This, in Kirk's view, is "the world of disorder, while what the conservative seeks to conserve is the world of order that we have inherited, if in a damaged condition, from our ancestors. The conservative mind and the ideological mind stand at opposite poles. And the contest between these two mentalities may be no less strenuous in the 21st century than it has been during the 20th."

The basic difference between conservatives and the advocates of the many ideologies which clutter the intellectual landscape—including some such as "libertarianism" and "neo-conservatism" which are often confused with conservatism—relates to the nature of man himself: "Man being imperfect, no perfect social order can be created. Because of human restlessness, mankind would grow rebellious under any utopian domination, and would break out once more in violent discontent or else expire of boredom. To seek for utopia is to end in disaster, the conservative says: 'We are not made for perfect things.' All that we can reasonably expect is a tolerably ordered, just, and free society, in which some evils, maladjustments and suffering will continue to lurk. By proper attention to prudent reform, we may preserve and improve the tolerable order. But if the old institutional and moral safeguards of a nation are neglected, then the anarchic impulse in mankind breaks loose . . . The ideologues who promise the perfection of man and society have converted a great part of the 20th century into a terrestrial hell."

A key element in prudential conservatism is the need to limit government power and divide it through a system of checks and balances. Yet, Kirk writes, "In every age . . . men and women are tempted to overthrow the limitations upon power, for the sake of some fancied advantage. It is characteristic of the radical that he thinks of power as a force for good—so long as the power falls into his hands. In the name of liberty, the French and Russian revolutionaries abolished the old restraints upon power; but power cannot be abolished. It always finds its way into someone's hands. That power which the revolutionaries had thought oppressive in the hands of the old regime became many times as tyrannical in the hands of the radical new masters of the state."

In a concluding epilogue addressed to young people, Kirk declares, ". . . as the century draws to its close, we may remind ourselves that ages of decadence in the past have been followed by ages of renewal." He urges the young to explore the past, discover the roots of our civilization and work to restore its sensibility. He concludes that, "Time is not a devourer only. With proper use of the life-span allotted to us, we may do much to redeem modernity from vices, terrors and catastrophic errors."

He quotes Orestes Brownson, who declared in 1843 that the scholar's mission was to "ask not what your age wants, but what it needs, not what it will reward, but what, without which, it cannot be saved, and that go and do . . ." For seventy five years, Russell Kirk has been doing just that, as this volume shows us so well.

—*Allan C. Brownfeld*

From Exclusion to Inclusion: The Long Struggle for African-American Political Power
Edited by Ralph C. Gomes and Linda Faye Williams
Greenwood Press Inc.
Westport, CT
pp 232
$45.00

A definitive reference book which is the outgrowth of a Howard University conference in 1989, *From Exclusion to Inclusion*, defines the historical evolution of the African-American voting right of 1870, the 15th U.S. Constitutional amendment, to the 90's projected influence of African-American elected officials on foreign policy.

Gomes and Williams examine historical barriers to African-American voter participation such as poll taxes, "grandfather clauses," and lynching. The book's editors pinpoint societal and state-by-state practices which led to the deterioration of the 15th amendment. These various actions, although illegal, were officially sanctioned throughout the southern states and led to the Voting Rights Act of 1965. Further examination of the evolution of African-American voting rights highlights the change in tactics by African-American political authorities from grassroots movements, such as marches and acts of civil disobedience, to coalition building and legislative influencing by lobbying groups.

Regarding foreign policy, Gomes and Williams provide perspective that directly correlates the increase in Congressional representation of African-Americans to United States policy toward the African diaspora. Gomes and Williams end with a look toward increasing voter participation by African-Americans and the significance of building political bridges with other minorities and divergent classes of white Americans.

From Exclusion to Inclusion is a collection of work which provides historical and timely accounts of the socio-political evolution of black Americans.

—*W. Yvette Parker*

Compassionate Capitalism
People Helping People to Help Themselves
by Rich DeVos
Penguin Books USA Inc. New York
336 pp $22.00

"I don't know the secret of success, but the secret of failure is trying to please everyone."
Bill Cosby

Nas Imran saw his dreams of professional football shattered when he got in with the wrong crowd. He ended up spending two years in state prison. After his release, he decided that what had happened to African-Americans could not be avenged; it had to be healed. He learned to forgive the past and dream great dreams.

Today, Nas owns a very successful Amway distributorship. Furthermore, he passed on his free enterprise ingenuity to hundreds of people who now own their own successful businesses. With his new financial security, Nas is free to spend his time, money and creativity to serve his community. The Amway Corporation uses part of its profits to support scholarships with the United Negro College Fund because Nas Imran and people like him dared to dream great dreams.

Rarely does an author of European ancestry write well deserved praise for great thinkers of African Ancestry. In his manifesto, *Compassionate Capitalism,* Amway founder Rich DeVos agrees with much of the philosophies of Marcus Garvey, Malcolm X, Booker T. Washington and Elijah Muhammad. Owning our own businesses, to supplement or replace our current income, is the best way to guarantee our personal freedom and to secure our family finances.

The reader is offered a penetrating examination of the historical and philosophical roots of modern free enterprise. Much of the book contains anecdotes about how people became prosperous as Amway distributors. Too little attention is paid to people who became prosperous without Amway. Nevertheless, the strategies DeVos provides for entrepreneurial success are applicable in almost any field.

As a child during the depression, his father taught him, "Own your own business, Rich. It's the only way to be free." After naming his business Amway (for "the American way"), Rich DeVos trumpeted the message of capitalism at churches and civic clubs. Today Amway prospers as a multibillion dollar corporation that even supports a charitable foundation.

While explaining how capitalism is the best way to help people, DeVos presents this strategy for wealth seekers:

1. Start saving
2. Get out of debt
3. Contribute to charitable causes even before you are out of debt.

DeVos defines entrepreneurism as a method of recognizing a human need then acting to fill it with courage, compassion and capital. Many people undertook the challenge of business ownership not only for financial gain but for human service. Becoming a compassionate capitalist begins with the decision that you can make a difference. Do you believe in yourself? Are you willing to at least try? If you can answer "Yes!" to these questions, then you are on the right track.

Rich DeVos compares the legacies of Adam Smith and Karl Marx. Capitalism has become the world's economic system of choice because it grants people the freedom to make a profit. During this century, it has been compassionate capitalists who have done more to meet the needs of the starving, homeless, sick and dying than all the socialists combined. When business people confront the facts of human needs, it is called marketing. Despite the fact that socialism is meant to share the wealth, in reality (as Lenin admitted), socialism quickly degenerates into the process of sharing the poverty.

Even though socialism had natural resources and human energy, it lacked compassion. The workers were owned by the state, the same as natural resources and tools. Since workers did not even own their own human energy, Soviet serfs lacked the motivation to get the job done. A century before Marx, Adam Smith advocated:

1. To succeed in business, liberate other people's talents.

2. Serve other people's needs and your needs will be met.

Like a professional economist, DeVos establishes a formula to explain his theories of Compassionate Capitalism. Below it is presented and explained.

$$MW = (NR + HE \times T) \times C$$

MATERIAL WELFARE (MW) Capitalism is the process of producing and distributing material (capital). You want to provide for your own material welfare and for those dependent upon your support. People strive to have a decent amount of material to make life happier.

NATURAL RESOURCES (NR) Directly or indirectly, every capitalist relies on the availability of natural resources. Occasionally, as quantities run low, an adequate substitute is discovered. Under capitalism, these precious assets of society tend to be privately owned. Local private ownership knows better what nearby people need and want. Distant big brother bureaucratic dictatorships prove to be poor custodians of natural resources.

HUMAN ENERGY (HE) By themselves, natural resources accomplish little. Human energy locates these supplies of potential wealth, prepares them and transforms them into more usable forms.

TOOLS (T) With the help of tools, human energy becomes so much simpler, cost-effective and productive.

COMPASSION (C) This guides us in our use of natural resources, human energy and tools. When compassion inspires free enterprise, profits follow because the quality of human life is advanced. Without compassion as an active ingredient, profits may temporarily follow, but the long term cost in human suffering will wipe out any gains.

Simply put, *our material welfare comes from natural resources that are transformed by human energy that has been made more effective through the use of tools all of which is enhanced by compassion.*

The Amway chairman even draws inspiration from people in the world of science. Hard working innovators have contributed immeasurably to improving human living conditions. For generations, chemists and physicists have applied a systematic approach to solving problems. Wanting to know what people wanted to buy, Thomas A. Edison adapted six business oriented rules in inventing products for the marketplace. He had no interest in creating inventions that would not sell.

1. Set a goal and stick to it.

2. Figure out the steps you have to go through to complete the invention (start a company) and follow them.

3. Keep good records of your progress.

4. Share your results with fellow workers.

5. Be sure that everyone working on the project (enterprise) has a clear definition of their responsibilities.

6. Record all your results for later analysis.

DeVos advocates developing a serious plan to guide our actions, both business and personal. We need to write down specific goals, stating when and how to achieve them. As we chart our progress, we will change course when necessary and celebrate when we accomplish our tasks.

Capitalism allows people to profit based on how well they serve others. During DeVos' term on President Reagan's AIDS Commission, he met a San Francisco grandmother who discovered her own power to make a difference. She realized that an AIDS stricken friend was too weak to prepare his own meals. Thereupon she founded Project Open Hand. Every morning at sunrise she would visit the local produce markets for "distressed" vegetables. After preparing meals in a church basement, she delivered them door to door to AIDS victims. Soon Project Open Hand grew into a charity serving eight thousand meals a day with an annual budget of nearly a million dollars. In the market place, people vote with their dollars. When the market votes "Yes!", capital is attracted to accomplish goals.

Free enterprise has proven itself to be the ladder by which poor people climbed out of their misery. Entrepreneurism is not a closed fraternity; anyone can join. Neither age, gender nor race is a barrier. Excessive regulations and bureaucratic red tape do form barriers. These hindrances thwart poor people from entering the business world.

At this time, Rich DeVos is busy underwriting a new foundation which, beginning in 1994, will award an annual Compassionate Capitalism Prize to individuals and institutions who are models of people helping people to help themselves. Try to be one of those people. You can write to the Compassionate Capitalism Foundation at P.O. Box 1233, Muskegon, MI 49443. It's the compassionate thing to do.

—*Cartrell Gore*

Above the Rim (R)

Here we go again. This is simply another street inspired flick, focusing on the malaise of our inner city communities, supposedly. It is undoubtedly entertaining. Duane Martin (Kyle) stars as a promising basketball player struggling with doing right or choosing the most unscrupulous path. Encouraging his immorality is Tupac Shakur depicted as a thug. Kyle's mother (Tonya Pickens) plays a dominant role in his life as well as just released prisoner and friend Marlon Wayans, who provided comic release. Acknowledging the exception of Kyle ultimately choosing the right path, this film, unfortunately never made it to the rim.

Written and produced by Barry Michael Cooper it takes place in Harlem.

Guarding Tess (PG-13)

I love politics and particularly The American Presidency, so of course, I saw this movie. I'm also a huge fan of Shirley MacLaine, who portrays an offensive, widowed former First Lady assigned Secret Service Protection. Agent Nicolas Cage bears the brunt of her special personality. She mistreats him badly initially but the two are inseparable before the end. The highlight was having the President interrupt his busy, busy schedule to dress down Cage when Shirley complained. Hilarious, well written and surely will take you for a loop.

Hugh Wilson stars as The President and is also the writer and director. This film takes place in a small midwestern town.

The Inkwell (R)

I thoroughly enjoyed this depiction of the 70s' dress, culture and confabulation. This movie was nicely executed. Supposedly, it takes place on the venerable Island of Martha's Vineyard. This is a story line about a teenager (Larenz Tate) coming of age. Larenz is a loner and claims a doll as his best and only friend. His family decided to visit relatives at the Vineyard as a way of getting away. Joe Morton plays his dad and Glynn Thurman plays the Uncle. Unfortunately, the focus was too much on his relationship with the opposite sex, which resulted in the loss of his purity. Nevertheless, it was a beautiful scene and for the most part a nice movie.

This movie was directed by Matty Rich.

—*Alvin Williams*